YORK NOTES

Macbeth

William Shakespeare

Notes by James Sale

 Longman   York Press

YORK PRESS
322 Old Brompton Road, London SW5 9JH

ADDISON WESLEY LONGMAN LIMITED
Edinburgh Gate, Harlow,
Essex CM20 2JE, United Kingdom
Associated companies, branches and representatives throughout the world

First published 1997

ISBN 0–582–31404–6

Illustrated by Gerry Grace
Designed by Vicki Pacey, Trojan Horse
Phototypeset by Gem Graphics, Trenance, Mawgan Porth, Cornwall
Produced by Longman Asia Limited, Hong Kong

ONTENTS

PREFACE

York Notes are designed to give you a broader perspective on works of literature studied at GCSE and equivalent levels. We have carried out extensive research into the needs of the modern literature student prior to publishing this new edition. Our research showed that no existing series fully met students' requirements. Rather than present a single authoritative approach, we have provided alternative viewpoints, empowering students to reach their own interpretations of the text. York Notes provide a close examination of the work and include biographical and historical background, summaries, glossaries, analyses of characters, themes, structure and language, cultural connections and literary terms.

If you look at the Contents page you will see the structure for the series. However, there's no need to read from the beginning to the end as you would with a novel, play, poem or short story. Use the Notes in the way that suits you. Our aim is to help you with your understanding of the work, not to dictate how you should learn.

York Notes are written by English teachers and examiners, with an expert knowledge of the subject. They show you how to succeed in coursework and examination assignments, guiding you through the text and offering practical advice. Questions and comments will extend, test and reinforce your knowledge. Attractive colour design and illustrations improve clarity and understanding, making these Notes easy to use and handy for quick reference.

York Notes are ideal for:
- Essay writing
- Exam preparation
- Class discussion

The author of these Notes is James Sale. James is an experienced teacher and has worked extensively with students on various examinations. He has been a head of drama and a head of English, as well as deputy headteacher in two schools with responsibility for assessment. He has been involved with nearly twenty educational books on poetry and drama.

The text used in these Notes is The New Penguin Shakespeare, revised edition, 1995.

Health Warning: **This study guide will enhance your understanding, but should not replace the reading of the original text and/or study in class.**

PART ONE

INTRODUCTION

HOW TO STUDY A PLAY

You have bought this book because you wanted to study a play on your own. This may supplement classwork.

- Drama is a special 'kind' of writing (the technical term is 'genre') because it needs a performance in the theatre to arrive at a full interpretation of its meaning. When reading a play you have to imagine how it should be performed; the words alone will not be sufficient. Think of gestures and movements.

- Drama is always about conflict of some sort (it may be below the surface). Identify the conflicts in the play and you will be close to identifying the large ideas or themes which bind all the parts together.

- Make careful notes on themes, characters, plot and any sub-plots of the play.

- Playwrights find non-realistic ways of allowing an audience to see into the minds and motives of their characters. The 'soliloquy', in which a character speaks directly to the audience, is one such device. Does the play you are studying have any such passages?

- Which characters do you like or dislike in the play? Why? Do your sympathies change as you see more of these characters?

- Think of the playwright writing the play. Why were these particular arrangements of events, these particular sets of characters and these particular speeches chosen?

Studying on your own requires self-discipline and a carefully thought-out work plan in order to be effective. Good luck.

Born in Stratford upon Avon in 1564, William
Shakespeare died there almost exactly fifty-two years
later, in 1616. During those fifty-two years he created
at least thirty-seven plays and possibly had a hand in
others. He was also to write several poems, including
his famous Sonnets (see Literary Terms).

He lived in an age when printing was commonplace,
yet most of his works were published either after his
death or without his authority. The lives of great people
were increasingly being written about, yet precious little
comment on Shakespeare survives from those years. As
we will see, this makes *Macbeth* the more striking: we
know that this play was written for a particular King at
a particular moment of history. Therefore, in studying
Macbeth we have some extra information. This,
perhaps, enables us to find some greater insight into the
art and mind of William Shakespeare.

Family Life   He came from yeoman's stock – his father, John
Shakespeare, was a farmer's son who became a
successful tradesman in Stratford, until he ran into
financial difficulties. His mother, Mary Arden, came
from a higher social class: her father was a member of
the gentry, and the owner of inherited property. This
is significant because Shakespeare aspired to be a
member of this class, and later on in life purchased a
coat of arms for his father. Such a purchase would
prove a sure sign of his being descended from
gentlemanly origins. If we remember that during much
of Shakespeare's life, the profession of acting was
synonymous with beggary and vagabondage, this is a
remarkable achievement.

Although no record exists, Shakespeare was almost
certainly educated at the local grammar school. He did
not, however, have a university education. What he did
after leaving school is unclear and several stories persist,
including the early one that 'he had been in his younger

yeares a Schoolmaster in the Countrey'. What we do know is that he had a relationship when he was eighteen with Anne Hathaway. She was eight years his senior and became pregnant. They married hastily in 1582 and their first child, Susanna, was born in 1583. They had two other children, twins, Judith and Hamnet, born in 1585. The period after this is called the 'dark years' because so little is known about his life until we find him in London as an actor and playwright.

Major works   Shakespeare appears to have been a well-liked and witty man – 'gentle' is perhaps the adjective that best describes him. As an actor he would appear to have been unexceptional. But as a playwright, learning his craft from the best writers of the period, such as Christopher Marlowe, he went on to become phenomenally successful. Plays like *Richard the Third*, *Romeo and Juliet*, the *Henry* plays, *The Merchant of Venice* and *Macbeth* were 'smash hits'. Initially, he was most successful with his history plays. Subsequently, he also wrote comedies, terminating in *Twelfth Night*. Towards the end of the reign of Elizabeth the First, his mood seems to have darkened and he wrote his great tragedies (see Literary Terms). In the final three or four years of his writing career, Shakespeare composed a number of 'pastoral romances' and a last history play. Two indications of how successful he was are shown by the fact that he not only acted in and wrote plays, but he also owned a stake in the theatre group, The King's Men, of which he was a part. Furthermore, the King's Men, were literally King James the First's men – the premier theatre group in the country, not only appearing before the public in their Globe Theatre, but also some dozen times or so a year giving private performances at court before the King and Queen. Such a private – indoor – performance for *Macbeth* is particularly suitable: the need in the play for darkness would be greatly facilitated by indoor exhibition.

When Shakespeare retired to live in Stratford for the final few years of his life, he was relatively speaking a rich man. His son, Hamnet, had died some years before, but both his daughters survived him, and both married and had children. Regrettably, all his grandchildren died without issue some time during the seventeenth century. In 1623, seven years after his death, his friends brought out the great First Folio edition of thirty-six of his plays. It was this which was to ensure his memory and his work lived on from generation to generation.

CONTEXT & SETTING

Many writers throughout history have composed their works for Kings, Queens or rich or important persons. This is called patronage.

Macbeth was written sometime between 1603 and 1606. This coincides with the accession of James the Sixth of Scotland to the English throne, as James the First of England, in 1603. The play was certainly written with James primarily in mind and there is a story that he 'was pleas'd with his own Hand to write an amicable letter to Mr Shakespeare'. Whether he wrote the letter to Shakespeare or not, the play certainly shows James is his focus in a number of ways.

First, it pays homage to the interests and expertise of James: its fascination with the supernatural courts his attention: witchcraft (Act I Scene 1, Act I Scene 3 and Act IV Scene 1), apparitions and ghosts (Act II Scene 1 and Act III Scene 4) and the King's Evil (Act IV Scene 3) were areas of great concern to James. He had even written a book, *Demonology*, on the subject.

Second, it compliments James by making his ancestor, Banquo, a hero in the play. As Duncan puts it: 'Noble Banquo,/Thou hast no less deserved' (I.4.30–1). Yet despite also receiving supernatural solicitation, he –

unlike Macbeth – does not fall into evil. Furthermore, as Macbeth admits, Banquo's is the greater spirit: 'under him/My genius is rebuked' (III.1.54–5). This is dramatically apt – but in point of fact, Banquo historically was an accomplice in the murder of Duncan. A reminder of this, presumably, would not have pleased James.

The Divine Right of Kings meant that because God appointed the King, the King was not answerable to the people or to Parliament.

Third, the play explores the issue of kingship and loyalty. These were of profound importance to James, who early in life had survived an assassination attempt. Moreover, his father, Lord Darnley, had been murdered and his mother, Mary Queen of Scots, had been executed as a traitor. Thus, questions of the role of the monarch and the duties of their subjects towards them, were ever in the forefront of his mind. Within the space of forty years, it was James's son, Charles the First, whose insistence upon the Divine Right of Kings led to the English Civil War and his own downfall and death.

Fourth, the play is intimately related to the topical events of the Gunpowder Plot of 1605 and the subsequent trials of its conspirators. This failed coup was sensational in a number of ways – the sheer audacity of blowing up Parliament amazed the country, as did the scale of the treachery involved. Shakespeare himself almost certainly knew some of the conspirators. Some were from Shakespeare's home county, Warwickshire. The discovery of the plot, late in the day, seemed 'miraculous' – James thought it so. And the trial itself cast Catholicism in a bad light: Father

A modern phrase which is now similar in meaning to 'equivocate' is 'being economical with the truth'.

Garnett defended 'equivocation', which meant that lies under oath were morally justified. Shakespeare picks up this theme in the play: Banquo talks of the 'truths' which betray us (I.3.123), and the Porter debates the equivocator who 'could not equivocate to heaven' (II.3.10–11). This is related to the wider theme of appearances. It was Lady Macbeth who advises

Macbeth to 'look like the innocent flower,/But be the serpent under't' (I.5.63–4).

It should be clear from the points concerning James the First that the world Shakespeare lived in was very different from today's. Of paramount importance was the political issue of succession and order. Shakespeare was born during the reign of Queen Elizabeth the First. Although Elizabeth would rule long and prosperously, this did not disguise the fact that there was an immense potential for subversion throughout her reign: the Tudor dynasty had successfully healed the wounds caused by the civil war known as the War of the Roses. However, it was not long after England had recovered from this dreadful event, that Henry the Eighth, Elizabeth's father, renounced the Roman Catholic faith and established the Church of England. This created a double problem for national unity. First, one of Henry's children, Mary, succeeded to the throne and forcibly

One final result of the struggle which is still true today is that no Catholic can become the Sovereign of Great Britian.

reestablished the Catholic faith. On Mary's death, her half sister, Elizabeth succeeded and reasserted the Protestant faith – the issue of belief, therefore, became one which threatened to divide the country once more. Second, alongside it, 'true' Catholic countries like Spain became the enemies of England – and until the defeat of the Spanish Armada in 1588 there was a real danger of invasion by Spain to restore Catholicism. The Gunpowder Plot itself was a last desperate gamble by the Catholics to reassert, as they saw it, the 'true' faith.

Shakespeare dedicated two poems to the Earl of Southampton, and many think he is also featured in Shakespeare's Sonnets.

Elizabeth remained the 'Virgin' Queen throughout her reign, which meant she had no natural successor. This created further instability – the Essex rising of 1601 in which Shakespeare's friend and patron, the Earl of Southampton was involved and imprisoned as a result, was a symptom of the need for political certainty – Elizabeth herself did not name her successor till she actually came to her death-bed.

The country, therefore, knew only too well the dire implications of insurrection and anarchy – such events were only too recent in their mind. And they had to be avoided in future – hence the importance of order, degree and loyalty. This order – hierarchy, even – had not only political but religious backing: God had created a world of order. We might now call it a 'pecking order'. We see a reference to it at Macbeth's feast. He invites his assembled guests to sit down: 'You know your own degrees' (III.4.1). Where one sits is determined by rank. By divine appointment, the King ruled over men and to violate or seek to violate this situation was against God's Will thereby producing 'unnatural' results. Thus, the unnatural killing of Duncan is accompanied by, amongst other things, 'A falcon [a sovereign bird] towering in her pride of place/Was by a mousing owl [an inferior bird] hawked at and killed [so, an unnatural event]' (II.4.12–13).

The question of whether witchcraft is 'real' is still relevant today. Films such as The Exorcist *reflect the popular belief that even in a scientific society there may be more to witchcraft than meets the eye.*

This question of 'unnaturalness' links thematically to the other striking aspect of *Macbeth*'s plot and staging: witchcraft. We must remember that England was not the industrial, scientific and urban society it largely is now. Belief in witchcraft and demonology was widespread. The objection to it – and in 1604 its practice became punishable by death – was precisely that it attempted to subvert God's natural order. We see this clearly in the Weird Sisters: females who have beards (I.3.45) and who in their spells invoke a 'birth-strangled babe/Ditch-delivered by a drab' (IV.1.30–1). They substitute death at the point of birth, and their major achievement is leading Macbeth (and many others) to destruction. Two key points for us are: how far do we see the supernatural in the play as psychological, and how far are the manifestations 'real'? The interpretation of these points is crucial for staging the play.

PART TWO

SUMMARIES

GENERAL SUMMARY

Act I:
Plans against
King Duncan

Three witches meet in a storm and plan to encounter Macbeth. King Duncan is told by a wounded captain and then by Ross how brave Macbeth and Banquo have defeated the Norwegian army and the Scottish rebels. He bids Ross inform Macbeth that he has gained the title Thane of Cawdor. The three witches await Macbeth and Banquo returning from the battle. They inform Macbeth he will be Thane of Cawdor and King of Scotland. They tell Banquo his descendants will be Kings. Soon after they disappear, Macbeth is officially informed that he has become the Thane of Cawdor. He reveals his hopes for the crown. Duncan personally thanks Macbeth and Banquo for their help and announces his son, Malcolm, heir apparent. Lady Macbeth, having received word from her husband, shares in his ambition, but worries that her husband is too kind to be able to take the throne. She calls on spirits to give her the strength to undertake the deed. When Macbeth arrives she praises him and insists on planning the murder of Duncan. Shortly, Duncan arrives at the Macbeth's castle where he is welcomed by Lady Macbeth.

Act II:
Action against
King Duncan

Macbeth wavers in his resolve to kill Duncan. But his wife cajoles him. As he goes to do it, he thinks he sees a dagger leading him on. After murdering Duncan, he returns to Lady Macbeth in a distraught, emotional state. He also inadvertently brings back the murder weapons. She upbraids him but he is too frightened to replace them on Duncan's drugged guards. Instead, Lady Macbeth goes and smears them with the blood and guilt. There is a knocking at the gate and they

retire to bed to pretend innocence. Macduff and
Lennox arrive to wake Duncan. Macduff exchanges
pleasantries with the Porter before Macbeth arrives,
who escorts Macduff to the entrance to Duncan's
chambers. Macduff finds Duncan murdered and the
alarm is sounded. Macbeth slays the guards in fury as
the main nobles, Lady Macbeth, and Duncan's two
sons, Malcolm and Donalbain, assemble. Macduff
challenges Macbeth's action in killing the guards, and
as Macbeth justifies his actions, Lady Macbeth faints.
In the ensuing confusion, Malcolm and Donalbain, for
fear of their lives, slip away to England and Ireland
respectively. Ross and an Old Man discuss how
unnatural these events have been. Macduff enters and
informs them that Macbeth will succeed to the throne,
although he will not attend Macbeth's coronation.

Act III:
Reign of King
Macbeth

The witches prophecy has come true for Macbeth.
Banquo suspects that Macbeth has 'playedst most
foully' for the crown. Macbeth, however, is seemingly
friendly with Banquo and invites him as chief guest to
his feast. As Banquo leaves, Macbeth reveals his fear
that the prophecy concerning Banquo might come true.
Thus, he entertains two murderers whom he instructs
to assassinate Banquo and his son, Fleance. Lady
Macbeth is isolated and not involved in the plan. She
attempts to lighten Macbeth's mood – they are both
restless and sleepless. Three murderers kill Banquo but
Fleance escapes. During the feast Macbeth twice sees
the ghost of Banquo focusing on him. He is completely
unnerved; only the quick thinking of Lady Macbeth
saves Macbeth from blurting out his guilt to those
assembled. She dismisses those present. In the
aftermath, Macbeth recovers himself and reveals he
intends to act against Macduff and also intends to visit
the three witches. The queen of the witches, Hecate,
bids them properly prepare for Macbeth's visit. Lennox

confides to another lord his suspicions concerning Macbeth. We learn that Macduff has fled to Malcolm at the English court.

Act IV:
Plans against
King Macbeth

Macbeth visits the witches and also meets their masters. He discovers that he should fear Macduff, but that nobody born of a woman can harm him. And also that he will reign until Birnan Wood comes to Dunsinane. To his chagrin, the prophecy relating to Banquo's offspring is confirmed. After leaving them, Macbeth finds Macduff is fled. He immediately orders the destruction of Macduff's whole family. Ross warns Lady Macduff, but it is too late: she and her son are murdered. In England, Malcolm tests Macduff – the true qualities of a king are discussed, particularly in the light of the saintly king of England's ability to cure the sick through the touch of his hands. Ross arrives and informs Macduff of the slaughter of his family. Malcolm informs Macduff that England will provide an army under Seyward to defeat Macbeth. Macduff vows personally to kill Macbeth.

Act V:
Actions
against King
Macbeth

Lady Macbeth is now ill: sleepwalking and talking in her sleep. Her doctor and gentlewoman realise the implications of the guilty things she is saying, but are impotent to cure her. The English army marches on Macbeth who fortifies his castle at Dunsinane and prepares for a siege. Malcolm orders the boughs of trees to be cut down and used as camouflage – hence anticipating the prophecy. Macbeth hears a scream and learns his wife has died – apparently by suicide – but he is unconcerned: his life appears to lack any meaning. However, he is enraged by the next message he receives: Birnan Wood is coming to Dunsinane. He abandons his siege plan and goes out fighting. His army is losing but nobody seems able to kill Macbeth: he kills Seyward's son in combat. Then he meets Macduff. They fight, but upon learning that Macduff is not born of a woman – he was born by Caesarean operation – he loses his courage and refuses to continue. Macduff baits him and they engage to the death – Macbeth is killed. Macduff produces the head of Macbeth for Malcolm and hails him King of Scotland. Malcolm invites all to attend his coronation at Scone.

DETAILED SUMMARIES

ACT I

SCENE 1

Why do you think we meet the witches first in the play?

In the middle of a storm three witches, sometimes called the Weird Sisters, meet. Their riddling rhymes indicate that they purpose shortly to encounter Macbeth.

COMMENT

The witches are highly ambiguous creatures – whether they are even human is debatable. To form a full picture you will need to study their appearances in Act I Scene 3 and Act IV Scene 1 (see also Characters). For now they create a sense of mystery: they will meet when 'the battle's lost and won' (line 4), which seems a contradiction.

The fact that they are evil is shown in their final couplet (see Literary Terms). According to them, 'Fair is foul, and foul is fair' (line 9). Put another way this means: good is bad and bad is good. The witches are violating God's natural order.

GLOSSARY   **Grey-Malkin, Padock** witches often had demon-companions called 'familiars' who followed them around. Usually, these familiars either assumed the shape of, or inhabited the body of an animal. Grey-Malkin is likely to be a cat; Padock possibly a toad.
Anon soon

SCENE 2   King Duncan and his court receive news from a wounded Captain that the battle against the traitor and rebel Macdonwald and his army was evenly balanced until Macbeth and Banquo in acts of outstanding courage and ferocity destroyed him and his troops. But as this occurs, reinforcements from the King of Norway and the traitor, the Thane of Cawdor, counterattack Macbeth and Banquo. However, these two are not at all dismayed; but as the Captain is taken away to tend his wounds, the outcome is still unsure. The Thane of Ross arrives to report that, through the fighting spirit of Macbeth, Duncan's army has won a great victory. Duncan declares that the traitor Thane of Cawdor is to be executed and Macbeth is to receive his title and estates as a reward.

COMMENT   From the shadowy world of the witches we switch to the immediate and physical world of battle and action.

What impressions do you form of Macbeth from comments about him so far?   Notice that we have not yet met Macbeth. The witches mention him earlier. Now the Captain and Ross do. Whilst the battle is primitive and bloody, yet their descriptions emphasise an heroic, even 'epic' quality about the proceedings, especially Macbeth's part in them. This is shown in the personifications (see Literary Terms) – 'Disdaining fortune' (line 17), 'valour's minion' (line 19), 'Bellona's bridegroom' (line 56) – and references: 'memorize another Golgotha' (line 41). Duncan himself generously praises Macbeth, and the final epithet (see Literary Terms) he gives is 'noble' (line 70).

The use of irony (see Literary Terms) – more specifically, dramatic irony (see Literary Terms) – is particularly important as this play explores the subtle distinctions between what is seemingly so and what actually is. A good example here is Duncan's comment that the Thane of Cawdor shall no more deceive him. He does not know, as we do, that when Macbeth becomes Thane of Cawdor he will also be a traitor. Ironically, it is in becoming the Thane of Cawdor that Macbeth's ambition to become king grows.

GLOSSARY   **kerns and galloglasses** light and heavily armed Celtic troops

unseam'd him from the nave to th' chops cut him open from his navel to his jaws (notice that the imagery – see Literary Terms – of 'seam' is that of clothing – this recurs in the play)

memorize another Golgotha make as memorable as Christ's death at Calvary

Bellona's bridegroom Macbeth – described as a fit husband for the Roman goddess of war, Bellona

lapped in proof clad in well-tested armour

confronted him with self-comparisons matched him point for point in skill and courage. But notice the irony: Macbeth will also match him point for point in treachery

craves composition wants terms to be agreed under a truce

SCENE 3   The storm still attends the three witches as they gather to boast of their exploits. They cast a spell as they prepare to meet Macbeth. He arrives with Banquo and both are shocked by the appearance of the witches. They greet Macbeth and inform him that he will become Thane of Cawdor and also King of Scotland. Whilst Macbeth is stunned by these prophecies, Banquo demands they inform him of his future. He is told that although he will not be King, his offspring will be. Macbeth recovers from his 'trance' and insists that the witches explain how they know these things, since they are frankly incredible. But the witches vanish as abruptly as they came.

Macbeth and Banquo briefly discuss the 'insane' revelations they have just heard, and at that point Ross and Angus arrive to convey thanks from King Duncan. Ross tells Macbeth he has become the Thane of Cawdor. Macbeth and Banquo are both amazed, and we begin to see Macbeth's ambition unfolding through the asides – or soliloquys (see Literary Terms) – he delivers to the audience. Banquo warns of the danger of trusting such supernatural messages, but Macbeth is lost in his own thoughts, thinking through all the implications. Eventually, he is stirred and agrees to ride towards the king. In private to Banquo, he suggests they speak about the revelations at some future point, which Banquo agrees to.

Soliloquys are a convention used in many plays of this period, not just Shakespeare's. They are a way of 'thinking aloud' to the audience.

COMMENT   The witches' boasting invokes evil but also reveals some limitations to their powers. They may have the power to change shape, but the rat has no tail (line 9) – in other words, is unnaturally and imperfectly formed. Furthermore, in their attack upon the 'master o' the *Tiger*' (line 7) they admit 'his bark cannot be lost' (line 24). What they do to him, however, is reminiscent of Macbeth's future condition: 'dry as hay' (line 18), sleepless (lines 19–20), and he will 'dwindle, peak, and pine' (line 23).

Macbeth's first words – 'So foul and fair a day I have not seen' (line 37) – echo the witches' words (I.1.9). This suggests he is already in tune with their way of thinking.

Banquo's description of the witches is important in seeing how unnatural they are: they seem to be women but are not. It is Banquo who thinks they are evil:

'What! Can the devil speak true?' (line 105). Macbeth does not.

Consider how responsible the witches are for what Macbeth subsequently does.

Note how keen Macbeth is to hear more of this 'strange intelligence' (line 74): 'Would they had stayed!' (line 81). This is exactly what he wants to hear and this can only be because they touch a nerve already present in Macbeth.

Banquo's warning to Macbeth concerning the 'instruments of darkness' (line 123) might also be construed as prophetic – Macbeth is betrayed as a result of believing these 'truths', and he comes to realise this in his final confrontation with Macduff (V.6.58–61).

The soliloquy (see Literary Terms) beginning 'Two truths are told' (line 126) shows that Macbeth all too quickly, following his accession as Thane of Cawdor, begins that process of imagining the steps he will need to take – that is, murdering Duncan – to become king. At this point the real horror of doing the deed seems to be balanced by a morbid fascination at its prospect.

The imagery (see Literary Terms) of clothing – 'borrowed robes' (line 108) and 'strange garments' (line 145) – begins to be developed. This is significant because clothing is a powerful image suggesting concealment and disguise: Macbeth, as it were, hides behind his clothes of kingship.

GLOSSARY

Aroint thee ... the rump-fed ronyon begone [as in exorcism] you ... the well-fed, mangy creature

penthouse lid eyelid

Weird sisters this name for the witches, which Macbeth himself uses (I.5.6 and III.4.132), suggests the Norse goddesses of destiny or fate – and hence fatality

Sinell's death Macbeth's father's death

insane root probably deadly nightshade, known to produce insanity

My thought, whose murder yet is but fantastical,/Shakes so my single state of man/That function is smothered in surmise,/And nothing is but what is not My thoughts, which are only imagining murder at the moment, so disturb my whole being that action is impossible because I am wholly focused on a future – when I shall be king – which does not yet exist

SCENE 4

Describe Duncan's relationship with his family and thanes.

King Duncan enquires of his son, Malcolm, about the execution of the Thane of Cawdor. He is told that Cawdor died repenting of his actions and with dignity. Macbeth and Banquo arrive and are profusely thanked by Duncan for their efforts. Duncan announces that his son, Malcolm, is to be his heir and also that he will visit Macbeth in his castle at Inverness. Macbeth leaves to prepare for the arrival of the King, but we learn that the announcement of Malcolm as heir is a bitter blow to him. If Macbeth is to be King, then this is something he must overcome. In his absence, Duncan praises Macbeth to Banquo.

COMMENT

The scene highlights a series of further contrasts: between Duncan and Banquo who are open and direct; and Macbeth who is covert in his intentions. Typically, for Duncan, stars shine (line 42), whereas for Macbeth they hide their fires so that darkness prevails (lines 51–2). We also hear of the former Thane of Cawdor's noble death; this contrasts with the living Thane of Cawdor's ignoble ambition. Again, it is ironic (see Literary Terms) that Duncan should comment concerning the former Thane of Cawdor that 'There's no art/To find the mind's construction in the face' (lines 12–13), since he so clearly fails to read what is in the new Thane of Cawdor's face. His trust of Macbeth leads to his death. The use of these contrasts serves to establish two contrary things: first, just how good and worthy a King Duncan is; second,

Y

just how appalling a crime it would be for Macbeth to murder him.

In this scene Macbeth's attitude to the murder has changed, even hardened. In Scene 3 the prospect, though desirable, was terrifying. His soliloquy (lines 49–54 – see Literary Terms) reveals a new determination to carry it through. The vocabulary has switched from polysyllabic abstractions to largely monosyllabic matter-of-factness. Couplets (see Literary Terms) clinch the sense of the line and the sense of inevitability about the deed Macbeth must do.

GLOSSARY   **That the proportion both of thanks and payment** that I could have repaid you according to your merit
The eye wink at the hand the eye must not see what the hand (which will commit the murder) is doing

SCENE 5

Identify the passages that show whether Macbeth or his wife is most in control.

Lady Macbeth reads a letter from her husband informing her of his success in battle and, more importantly, of his encounter with the witches. He believes their knowledge to be true, and communicates his excitement about his eventual destiny to be King – and so for her to be Queen. After reading the letter, she is worried that Macbeth is too soft a person to be able to take the crown. She determines that she will assist him through the 'valour of my tongue' (line 25). On hearing – to her great surprise and then delight – that the King himself will be staying in their castle overnight, she exults and invokes demonic spirits to harden her own resolve and to destroy any weakness of pity. Macbeth enters and she immediately sets to work upon his intentions. He says little but she insists that the deed must be done, that she will personally organise its operation, and finally that failure to accomplish this act would be a form of fear.

PLANS AGAINST KING DUNCAN

COMMENT   Lady Macbeth immediately understands the full
implications of her husband's letter and her response is
direct and uncompromising: her husband must be what
he has been promised. No niceties of conscience or
loyalty seem to assail her, and it is noticeable how she
overwhelms her husband when he appears. It is also
interesting to reflect how she instantly taps into the
spirit world: her spirits (an interesting plural) will
invade Macbeth's ear, and she literally does invoke

Usually a person   spirits to possess her body. The point about her
has one spirit, but 'unsex'-ing and her 'woman's breasts' no longer being
'possession'   used for milk but murder, bares a curious parallel with
involves many.   the ambiguous sexuality of the witches themselves. It is
as if, at this level of evil, one abandons being either
male or female – one is a neutral 'it'. Later (I.7.46),
Macbeth himself, in trying to deflect his wife's
arguments, puts forward the view that in daring/doing
more than what is proper – or natural – for a man to
do, one no longer a man. Despite his argument, he,
of course, does precisely that.

The letter to Lady Macbeth shows not only complete
trust in his wife – for such a letter could itself be
construed as treasonous – but also affection and love:
'my dearest partner of greatness' (lines 9–10) suggests a
warm equality of persons.

We have already seen the bloody nature of battle in
Scene 2. The imagery (see Literary Terms) of blood
runs through the play. Look at what Lady Macbeth
requests: 'Make thick my blood' (line 41). Here blood is
seen as a natural function of the human body, and one
that naturally feeds man's capacity for compassion and
repentance – things she wishes stopped.

GLOSSARY   **missives** messengers
            illness wickedness

That which cries, 'Thus thou must do' if thou have it,/And that which rather thou dost fear to do/Than wishest should be undone the crown itself cries out 'You must do this' if you want to have the crown, and although you may fear to do it, you still want the crown whether or not you actually perpetrate the deed

golden round the crown (a figure of speech called synecdoche see Literary Terms). The crown itself is metonymic (see Literary Terms) as it stands for sovereignty/kingship.

unsex me remove from me the weakness of being a woman. We see this traditional view of women's incapacity for murderous activities in Macduff's remark to her (II.3.80–3).

make thick my blood prevent pity flowing through my veins

compunctious visitings of nature natural feelings of compassion

gall a bitter and unpleasant liquid

pall cloak

all-hail hereafter the kingship which has been foretold

SCENE 6

King Duncan arrives at Macbeth's castle with his sons and attendant thanes. He admires the air. Lady Macbeth – without her husband – greets Duncan and they exchange pleasant courtesies. Duncan takes her hand and is led into the castle.

COMMENT

Note that Macbeth was not present to greet King Duncan.

Once more the theme of reality versus appearances is lightly alluded to. The air and the castle appear delightful, but are in reality to be the site of foul murder.

Ironically, Duncan refers to Macbeth as the 'Thane of Cawdor'.

GLOSSARY

pendent bed and procreant cradle suspended place of rest and place of birth

The love that follows us sometimes is our trouble,/Which still we thank as love love sometimes causes me trouble but despite that I thank it as love

God 'ield us God reward us

we rest your hermits we shall continue to pray for you

purveyor forerunner

in compt/To make their audit subject to account to make their examination (of them)

SCENE As Macbeth's household prepares the feast for Duncan, Macbeth, alone, debates the pros and cons of murdering Duncan in his own mind. The biggest problem as he sees it is that murdering his own liege, kinsman and guest would set a precedent that would return to plague him. Also, he cannot dismiss the fact that Duncan has been such a good king – heaven itself will expose the wickedness of Macbeth. The only justification for the murder is, finally, his own ambition. His wife enters and he informs her he intends to change his mind and not murder Duncan – why should he throw away all the glory he has so recently gained? She is contemptuous of his change of heart and accuses him of cowardice. They argue but her violent resolution prevails – she outlines the plan – and he agrees to it.

COMMENT

What is Macbeth's most powerful reason for not murdering Duncan?

Macbeth – his guilt isolating him, and in some anguish as he seeks to decide what to do – reasons that if he could get away with the murder, then he wouldn't worry about damnation in the after-life. However, the imagery (see Literary Terms) of his own imagination undermines his reasonings: as he considers Duncan's virtuous qualities, pictures of angels and cherubims seeking retribution assail and frighten him. Again, ironically (see Literary Terms), the initial hope that one blow would end the matter (lines 4–5) proves utterly false: the death of Duncan is swiftly followed by the illegal 'execution' of the two innocent guards.

Lady Macbeth attacks her husband exactly where she knows it will hurt: his courage and manhood are at stake. And she does what she said she would do in Act I Scene 5, 'pour my spirits in thine ear' (lines 23–4). Her strength of purpose and her leadership offer a remarkable contrast to Macbeth's performance at this stage. Notice how his final words in this scene, 'False face must hide what the false heart doth know', echo Lady Macbeth's earlier advice (I.5.61–4).

GLOSSARY

trammel up prevent

his surcease Duncan's death

heaven's cherubim, horsed/Upon the sightless curriers of the air heaven's angels riding on the wind

the ornament of life kingship

Letting 'I dare not' wait upon 'I would'/Like the poor cat i'the adage letting fear control desire, just as the cat wanted to eat fish but was afraid to get her feet wet

Did then adhere did then provide an opportunity (to murder Duncan)

wassail carousing

That memory … A limbeck only their memory will become completely confused and their reason lack any substance

spongy drunken

quell kill

corporal agent fibre of my being

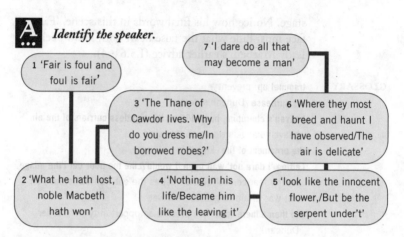

A *Identify the speaker.*

1 'Fair is foul and foul is fair'

2 'What he hath lost, noble Macbeth hath won'

3 'The Thane of Cawdor lives. Why do you dress me/In borrowed robes?'

4 'Nothing in his life/Became him like the leaving it'

5 'look like the innocent flower,/But be the serpent under't'

6 'Where they most breed and haunt I have observed/The air is delicate'

7 'I dare do all that may become a man'

Identify the person 'to whom' this comment refers.

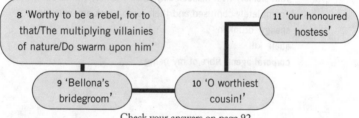

8 'Worthy to be a rebel, for to that/The multiplying villainies of nature/Do swarm upon him'

9 'Bellona's bridegroom'

10 'O worthiest cousin!'

11 'our honoured hostess'

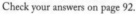

Check your answers on page 92.

B *Consider these issues.*

a How the witches interest the reader or playgoer at the beginning of the play.

b What treachery means and how it operates.

c The development of Macbeth's character and what we learn about him from his soliloquys (see Literary Terms).

d How important a partner can be in making decisions and which partner is the stronger character.

e How appearances can be deceptive.

f Whether knowing the future is a good idea and how it can influence someone.

g What reasons Macbeth has for not committing murder and treason.

sᴄᴇɴᴇ 1 Banquo is out walking late with his son, Fleance. He cannot sleep and feels some premonition that something is wrong. He encounters Macbeth and presents him with a diamond for Macbeth's wife, a gift from the King. He tells Macbeth that he dreamt of the witches. Macbeth dismisses thoughts of them, but requests that he and Banquo speak about the matter another time. Banquo agrees but not without the reservation that honour should not be comprised. Macbeth is left alone and imagines he sees a dagger in front of him – a dagger which guides him towards the goal he seeks of killing Duncan. Initially he experiences horror at the reality of what he is contemplating, but this gives way to resolution. As the bell rings, he determines to proceed forward and kill Duncan.

Cᴏᴍᴍᴇɴᴛ The introduction of Banquo at this point allows us another point of contrast with Macbeth. We see the witches have affected him too – but whereas Macbeth has surrendered his will to them, Banquo's dreams are invaded. Banquo senses something is wrong, but he does not know what. His openness, though, in admitting his feelings is in stark contrast to Macbeth, who flatly lies that he doesn't think about the witches. The gift of the diamond, too, especially to Lady

ACTION AGAINST KING DUNCAN

Banquo seems disturbed by recent events; consider if there is anything he should have done. Think about this again, when you have studied III.1.

Macbeth, underlines further the monstrous ingratitude of Macbeth himself, and rams home another irony (see Literary Terms): that Duncan has failed again to read 'the mind's construction in the face' (I.4.12–14), for it is Lady Macbeth who has ensured he is to be killed.

Macbeth's request to talk of the witches later with its promise to 'make honour for you' (line 26) is an attempt to sound Banquo out – how will he react should the status quo change? Banquo's answer, which insists upon maintaining integrity, is hardly likely to please Macbeth. Banquo cannot be bought. It is not surprising that later (III.1.51) Macbeth comments that he feels 'rebuked' by him.

GLOSSARY

largess to your offices gifts to your servants

Our will became the servant to defect,/Which else should free have wrought our intention to provide suitable hospitality for the king was thwarted

my bosom franchised and allegiance clear my being free from evil and my loyalty to the king uncompromised

sensible/To feeling as to sight capable of being touched as well as seen

heat-oppressèd fevered

Mine eyes are made the fools o' the other senses,/Or else worth all the rest either my eyes are fooled by seeing a dagger which does not exist, or else they are providing me with more significant information – i.e. leading me to what I have to do

dudgeon handle

gouts drops

prate tell

SCENE 2

Nerves on edge, Lady Macbeth waits for Macbeth to return from having done the murder. Her mood is exultant and bold, and she boasts how she has drugged the guards. She would have murdered Duncan herself, except his sleeping form reminded her of her father. Macbeth enters, shattered and slightly hysterical. He is

carrying two bloodstained daggers. He is obsessed by
the noises he has heard, and particularly is distressed by
the fact that when passing Malcolm and Donalbain's
chamber he was unable to say 'amen' in response to
their request for blessing. The guilt of what he has done
torments him, and Lady Macbeth attempts to allay and
rationalise his fears. She focuses on the need to keep to
the plan of action – ordering him to go back and place
the daggers beside the guards, so as to incriminate
them. Macbeth, however, is too terrified to return.
Lady Macbeth undertakes the deed and leaves him
there alone. A knocking at the castle gate further
disturbs his state of mind. Lady Macbeth reenters. As
the knocking continues she advises that he pulls himself
together and that they retire to bed, so as not to be seen
up and about when the murder is discovered.

COMMENT   We do not see the actual murder on stage. Instead,
prior to the murder we are made most aware of the
vision of the dagger leading Macbeth on; and after the
murder we are most conscious of sounds which disturb
the peace. The murder is, as it were, sandwiched
between intense sensory experiences – we are meant to
'feel' it happening.

Lady Macbeth is clearly – despite some nervous
apprehension – entirely in control of herself and of her
husband. She planned the execution, and now it is her
readiness of mind and strength of purpose that
compensates for Macbeth's failure to act decisively once
the murder is committed.

Irony (see Literary Terms) is ever present. Lady
Macbeth imagines that washing one's hands will wash
away guilt: it is she, finally (V.1.42), who is unable to
wash her hands clean. And her comment to Macbeth,
'Infirm of purpose!' (line 52), comes back to haunt her,
as he strengthens in evil resolve, whilst she becomes

madly suicidal – anticipated in her dismissive comment 'so, it will make us mad' (line 34).

The fact that such a great warrior – and killer of men – is so lost in terrifying guilt indicates the full extent of the evil he has committed. Earlier in the play, Macbeth wanted to 'jump the life to come' (I.7.7) – as if there were no divine retribution he need worry about. Now, the need for 'amen', which he cannot speak and the fact that even the ocean cannot clean him, suggests a state of total damnation.

GLOSSARY

mock their charge betray their responsibility (to protect the king)

hangman's hands in cases of treason, hanging also involved drawing and quartering the victim hence, the hangman's hands would be extremely bloody

ravelled sleave tangled skein

gild paint golden, as in the sense of embellish. There is a pun (see Literary Terms) with the following word 'guilt' which conveys a sense of jokiness, entirely inappropriate to the critical situation they are in, but necessary in terms of Lady Macbeth's efforts to lighten the awful weight of guilt Macbeth is experiencing

multitudinous seas incarnadine countless masses of water turn blood-red

the green one red the green sea a red sea

constancy firmness (has left you)

SCENE 3

The knocking from the previous scene continues and a porter, hungover from the night's feast, goes to open the gate. As he does so, he imagines he is the porter of hell. He lets in Macduff and Lennox. Seemingly awoken by their knocking, Macbeth comes forward to greet them. Macduff asks to be led to the King. While he enters the King's chamber, Lennox comments to Macbeth on how stormy the night was. Macduff, discovering the murder, returns, loudly proclaiming

treason. As Macduff proceeds to stir the castle,
Macbeth and Lennox rush in to ascertain the facts for
themselves. Lady Macbeth appears, then Banquo, and
both are informed of the reason for the commotion.
Macbeth returns and emotionally bemoans the dreadful
deed. At this point Malcolm and Donalbain arrive and
are informed rhetorically by Macbeth, and then directly
by Macduff, that their father's been murdered. Lennox
suggests the guards may have been responsible, and it
emerges Macbeth immediately slew them. Macduff
questions this, and as Macbeth justifies his actions, his
wife faints and attention is distracted to her. Banquo
assumes command and directs them to meet in
readiness. As they exit from stage, Malcolm and
Donalbain remain: they decide to flee – suspecting
treachery from someone closely related.

COMMENT   The bleak intensity of the previous scene gives way to a
brief comic interlude. Although the Porter is crude and
rough, and his introduction is intended to make us
laugh, yet his role also performs other important
functions. The continuation of physical knocking
reminds us that we are still in the world where the
Macbeths commit murder. Therefore, the Porter's self-
appointed role as a hell-porter is not so fanciful. Earlier
we have seen references to serpents (I.5.64) and chalices
(I.7.11) and with that the suggestion that the devil has
entered into Macbeth. Later, Macduff is to say that
Macbeth is a devil (IV.3.56). Literally, then, it would
seem, there is hell where Macbeth is. And, more
interestingly still, much of the Porter's speeches are
connected to contemporary events: namely, the
gunpowder plot and its own enormity of treason. Thus,
whilst making some good-humoured jokes, the overall
thrust of the Porter's remarks is to widen the
application of the play – hell is not only on the stage in
Macbeth's castle, but present in the society for which

Shakespeare was writing. Furthermore, we should not forget that we know that the murder has been committed – this delay in its discovery heightens the tension and our sense of anticipation.

Lennox's account of the storm is counterpointed by an almost dismissive four word reply (line 57) from Macbeth. In that tiny detail we see how unable Macbeth is to be natural and sociable – he has no time for ordinary conversation – he is keyed up and waiting for the outburst he knows must come from Macduff.

Typically, in a world of inverted values, Lady Macbeth's first concern on 'learning' that Duncan has been murdered is that it reflects badly on 'our house' (line 85). Equally typically, it is Banquo who provides a more sensitive perspective.

Killing the guards was not part of Lady Macbeth's original plan.

It can be argued that Macbeth's justification for killing the two guards becomes so colourful and rhetorical that he is in danger of being exposed through what might be considered 'overacting' his part. Lady Macbeth's swoon, therefore, at this point conveniently distracts attention away from her husband and the question he poses (lines 113–5). Perhaps, from his point of view, it were best left unanswered.

Donalbain and Malcolm's decision to flee clearly plays into Macbeth's hand. However, that does not mean it was a bad decision. To have stayed may well have led to their own assassinations. As they observe, the 'nea'er in blood/The nearer bloody' (lines 137–8). This can only mean they suspect Macbeth.

GLOSSARY   **old** more than enough

equivocator perjurer here specifically relating to the lies that the Jesuit, Henry Garnet, made under oath during his trial for his part in the gunpowder plot. Garnet went under the false name

y

of 'Farmer', so there is a punning (see Literary Terms) link
between the farmer and the equivocator

roast your goose heat your smoothing iron, but with an extra
sense of catch venereal disease – the point of all these
examples is that the farmer, the equivocator, and the tailor all
overreach themselves

nose-painting drinking paints the nose red

equivocates him in a sleep stirs lechery in him in sleep (through
dreams)

I made a shift to cast him I threw drink off by vomiting

The Lord's anointed temple the King, and here a reference to a
favourite idea of King James that the King was anointed by
God. Regicide, therefore, was not only a sin against mankind,
but against God himself.

The expedition of my violent love/Outrun the pauser reason the
strength of my love for Duncan meant (when I saw his
murdered body) that my powers of reason were suspended (so
I killed the murderers without proper trial)

Unmannerly breeched with gore improperly covered with clotted
blood

Hid in an auger-hole concealed by treachery in a tiny
hole (literally, a hole made by a sharp point such as a
dagger)

naked frailties state of undress (they need to clothe themselves
properly)

undivulged pretence purpose as yet unrevealed

SCENE 4   Ross and an Old Man recall the dreadful night of the
murder. The Old Man states that he cannot remember
a parallel to it. As they discuss the unnatural state of
things, darkness indeed seems to have usurped the place
of light. Macduff enters and brings them up to date
with the news. Duncan's two sons are suspected of
paying the guards to commit the murder precisely
because they have now fled. Macbeth has been
nominated King and has gone to Scone to be invested.
Ross asks Macduff whether he will go to the

investiture. Macduff says he will not, but will return home to Fife. Ross himself intends to go. They all part and the Old Man pronounces a blessing.

COMMENT   The scene gives us a breathing space before we meet the new King, Macbeth; and further, it acts as a commentary on all that has happened. The importance of the Old Man lies simply in his being a representative of the people, and one whose memory goes back a long way – the crimes committed are without parallel. Ross describes the extent of the darkness and this again symbolically (see Literary Terms) reminds us of Christ's crucifixion and the great darkness that enveloped the land.

Note Macduff's integrity.   Macduff's suspicions concerning Macbeth are revealed by two facts: the dry observation that the murderers were 'Those that Macbeth hath slain' (line 22) – and so could not be questioned – and that he will not go to Scone for the coronation. This contrasts with Ross's readiness to go and to align himself with the new regime.

GLOSSARY   **suborned** bribed to do evil

Scone historic site where the Kings of Scotland were traditionally crowned

Colmkill Iona – early place of burial for Scottish Kings

Lest our old robes sit easier than our new for our old King is likely to be more lenient than our new one – notice the clothing imagery (see Literary Terms) again

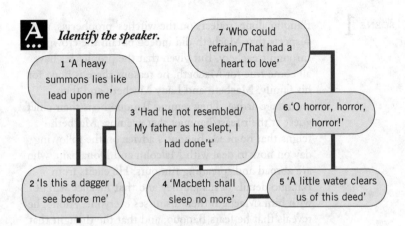

A *Identify the speaker.*

1 'A heavy summons lies like lead upon me'

2 'Is this a dagger I see before me'

3 'Had he not resembled/ My father as he slept, I had done't'

4 'Macbeth shall sleep no more'

5 'A little water clears us of this deed'

6 'O horror, horror, horror!'

7 'Who could refrain,/That had a heart to love'

Identify the person 'to whom' this comment refers.

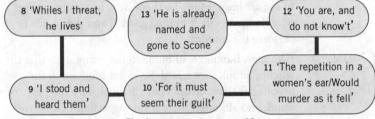

8 'Whiles I threat, he lives'

9 'I stood and heard them'

10 'For it must seem their guilt'

11 'The repetition in a women's ear/Would murder as it fell'

12 'You are, and do not know't'

13 'He is already named and gone to Scone'

Check your answers on page 92.

B *Consider these issues.*

a The effects of dreams and visions on the conscious mind.

b How the murder of Duncan is controlled by Lady Macbeth.

c Whether the Porter's comments are relevant to the play.

d What the effect of murdering Duncan has on the Macbeths' next actions.

e Whether Malcolm and Donalbain were wise to flee.

f How nature responds to evil when it occurs in the world.

g How Macduff responds to events.

Act III

SCENE 1

Banquo alone, reflects on the witches' prophecies, and suspects that Macbeth did indeed obtain the crown through treachery. But given that the prophecies have all come true for Macbeth, he reasons there is hope for his family. Macbeth and Lady Macbeth and their entourage arrive. They remind Banquo he is their chief guest at their feast/banquet that evening. Macbeth feigns that he needs Banquo's advice on the following day on how to deal with Malcolm and Donalbain, who are abroad and spreading rumours. He elicits from Banquo details of his journey and that Fleance will be with him. Macbeth then dismisses everyone. Alone, he reveals that he fears Banquo, and that the thought that Banquo's offspring should become Kings is entirely unacceptable to him. Two murderers whom he wishes to see are brought in. To them he vehemently outlines why Banquo is their mutual enemy, and they agree to perform the murder.

COMMENT

Although Banquo is immune to the temptation that the witches' prophecies afford, he is not immune to the prophecies themselves. They clearly disturb his peace of mind, and although there is no suggestion that he will 'help' the prophecies come true (as Macbeth did), he nevertheless begins to incline towards their 'truth'. This contrasts – in the same scene – with Macbeth's obsession that they will come true, and therefore that he (Macbeth) must stop them. A small irony (see Literary Terms) here is that Macbeth chooses the wrong course of action, since no child of Banquo can succeed while Banquo is alive.

Macbeth's comments on Banquo later in this scene give us much information about the character of Banquo: what emerges is his courage, wisdom and integrity.

This is the first time we see Macbeth as King. Immediately we discover the kind of King he is going to be: entirely duplicitous – the appearance of an innocent flower, but really the serpent under it (I.5.64-5). Under the guise of appearing to honour and value his erstwhile comrade-in-arms, he casually ascertains his movements that night and confirms that Fleance will be with him. All this to entrap and murder him and his child.

Compare the arguments used by Macbeth and Lady Macbeth when persuading murderers to kill.

The depths to which Macbeth has sunk are clear in his conversation with the murderers: here is a great warrior-hero – 'Bellona's bridegroom' (I.2.56) – who now has to meet the most vicious and corrupt kind of men in secret in order to both disguise and obtain his ends. The fact that he himself despises these men is shown in the way he addresses them – the interruption of the first murderer's solemn declaration of loyalty with the ironic 'Your spirits shine through you' (line 127) points to contempt. Subsequently, the mission of the third murderer (III.3) shows how little he actually trusts the first two. But, then, trust is no longer something Macbeth believes in. Crucially, in the next scene (III.2), even Lady Macbeth is not privy to his plans.

It is worth noting the bestial imagery (see Literary Terms): men can be classified in the same way as dogs. We remember that before he 'fell', Macbeth said he dared do all that a man should do – to do more was to be no man (I.7.47-8). In other words, acting like an animal is a natural consequence of his choices – and the imagery demonstrates that.

GLOSSARY   **all-thing** wholly

Go not my horse the better if my horse isn't fast enough

strange invention imaginative fabrications – suggesting Macbeth was the murderer

My genius is rebuked my spirit is intimidated or checked

unlineal not descended from me

rancours in the vessel poison in the cup

mine eternal jewel my immortal soul

the common enemy of man Satan, the devil

come fate into the list/And champion me to the utterance
  challenge fate to a duel to the death

passed in probation discovered the proof

Shoughs, water-rugs, and demi-wolves shag-haired dogs, rough-
  haired water dogs, and half-breed wolf dogs

valued file list where each appears according to its value

near'st of life vital parts

do make love entreat your help

SCENE 2

Lady Macbeth is attempting to comfort her husband. Do you feel any pity – even pathos – for either of them?

Lady Macbeth wants to speak to her husband before the feast. She is not happy – uncertainty and insecurity trouble them both. Macbeth appears and she upbraids him for both staying alone and for his continual dwelling on the actions they have done. Macbeth envies the peaceful dead. Lady Macbeth attempts to cheer him up. They discuss the feast ahead, resolve to praise Banquo at it, and then Macbeth reveals his fear of Banquo and Fleance. He then further reveals that he intends to commit another dreadful crime. He will not tell her what it is, but asks her to praise it when it's achieved. Lady Macbeth is amazed but drawn along with him.

COMMENT

In the encounters so far, Lady Macbeth has been dominant. Now we see the situation changing. Macbeth is keeping himself to himself and brooding on the crimes committed, and on the crimes he intends to commit – notice the bestial imagery (see Literary Terms) again: 'O, full of scorpions is my mind' (line 35). Furthermore, he is not sharing his thoughts with his 'dearest partner of greatness' (I.5.9-10) and so she herself is feeling isolated. This despite the affectionate term – 'dearest chuck' (line 45) – Macbeth uses for her.

For Macbeth this proves an incubation period in which he grows stronger – 'Things bad begun make strong themselves by ill' (line 55) – and inures himself to doing evil; for Lady Macbeth it is the start of her disintegration – she will take control one more time, at the banquet (III.4), and then she will be overwhelmed by remorse for the tide of evil she has helped unleash, and go mad. Their roles are reversing.

GLOSSARY   **let the frame of things disjoint** let the whole universe collapse
both the worlds suffer heaven and Earth perish
restless ecstasy frenzy of delirium
foreign levy army of foreign mercenaries
present him eminence honour him
Unsafe the while that we/Must lave our honours in these flattering streams while we are living in this unsafe time, we must keep our honour clean by washing it in flattery
shard-borne dung borne as well as borne aloft on scaly wings
seeling blinding (in the sense that a falcon's eyes are sewn up while it is being trained)
that great bond that great moral law, specifically prohibiting murder

SCENE 3   The two murderers are joined by a third. They await Banquo and Fleance's approach, spring out and manage to assassinate Banquo. In the confusion Fleance escapes. The murderers resolve to inform Macbeth of what's been done.

COMMENT   The addition of a third murderer adds nothing to the progress of the plot, but is a wonderful device for exposing the kind of world Macbeth inhabits and is further creating all around himself. Macbeth trusts no-one, not even the accomplices he has commissioned. In the next scene (III.4) we learn he has spies everywhere – everyone is being checked.

Notice the night and day contrasts which run through the play. The loss of light foreshadows the loss of life.

he needs not our mistrust we do not need to distrust the third murderer

the direction just just as Macbeth instructed us

note of expectation list of expected guests

let it come down the rain, but here the literal rain of Banquo's blood

SCENE 4

Macbeth welcomes various guests to his banquet. The first murderer appears and Macbeth steps aside to speak with him. He learns that Banquo is dead, but that Fleance escaped – this disturbs him. He returns to the feast and is gently upbraided by his wife for his absence.

Consider whether Banquo's ghost is real, or the product of Macbeth's guilty imagination.

As he stands, making a speech praising Banquo, Banquo's ghost takes the only remaining chair. Only Macbeth can see the ghost and he is terrified – only Lady Macbeth's quick thinking covers up the fact that Macbeth is beginning to reveal his guilt. The ghost disappears and Macbeth regains his composure. Once more he attempts good cheer and invokes the name of Banquo: the ghost reappears and Macbeth loses his nerve altogether. He recovers himself when the ghost disappears again, but too late to enable the banquet to continue. Lady Macbeth heads off a question from Ross and dismisses everyone. Alone with his wife, Macbeth confides that Macduff seems to be standing against him. He reveals, too, that he has spies everywhere, and that he intends to revisit the witches.

COMMENT   This scene raises the interesting question of witchcraft and psychology. Certainly, the supernatural motif (see Literary Terms) is superbly developed: we have had the witches, their prophecies, the dagger that led Macbeth to Duncan, and now we have the ghost of Banquo. But whereas Banquo saw and heard the witches alongside Macbeth, here only Macbeth sees the vision. As Lady Macbeth says, 'When all's done/You look but on a stool' (line 65-6). This has practical implications for any production of the play – is the ghost in the mind of Macbeth solely (and so is not shown on stage), or does a ghost really appear? Perhaps because of its sheer dramatic impact, most versions of the play tend to want to show the ghost!

The dramatic tension in this scene is brilliantly exploited. First, the appearance of the murderer (albeit on the fringes) is itself shocking – perhaps one needs to consider this in modern terms: it would be like a street gangster appearing in the doorway of a State banquet. The risks to Macbeth in being seen with such a person are enormous – and this gives a clear indication of his state of mind. Macbeth *has* to know that Banquo and Fleance are dead, whatever the consequences. As he says later in the scene: 'For mine own good/All causes shall give way' (lines 134–5). Second, the tension is exploited by the way that Macbeth in fact reveals – almost plainly – his guilt, but on each occasion Lady Macbeth is able ingeniously to bale him out. We are kept on tenterhooks: will he be exposed? And she just manages to keep him ahead of it.

Having taken such enormous risks in becoming King, Macbeth now desires complete certainty – he 'has' to know.

The strain on Lady Macbeth is evident. Although he himself has been terrified, Macbeth, by the end of the

scene, seems casual in his attitude to what has
happened. His comment, 'We are yet but young in
deed' (line 143) suggests that this mere blip will soon
pass. She, however, has had to use all her resources and
wit to contain the potential damage of exposure. Earlier
she had said 'Naught's had, all's spent' (III.2.5) and we
see this particularly in this scene: she wanted to be
Queen and the scene begins with her keeping 'her state'
(line 5), in other words, remaining on her throne. If
there was anywhere in the play where the full
enjoyment of majesty could be entertained, it is here:
Lady Macbeth on her throne, surrounded by subjects.
Yet this, through Macbeth's actions becomes a hollow
and empty event, lacking any dignity or regal
significance. Perhaps no wonder, lacking any other
significance in her life, her mind then does begin to
question the value of what it has accomplished.
Macbeth, we notice, no longer talks of the *we* – himself
and his partner of greatness – but of himself alone: 'For
mine own good/All causes shall give way' (lines 134–5).

Banquo's ghost, ironically (see Literary Terms),
occupies Macbeth's seat – as his descendants will his
throne – 'push us from our stools' (line 81).

The reference once more to sleep (line 140) reinforces
our sense of their guilt, but also points to the dramatic
irony (see Literary Terms) that Macbeth himself is a
prophet: 'Macbeth shall sleep no more' (II.2.43).

GLOSSARY   **Both sides are even** two possible meanings: the guests have
             returned Lady Macbeth's welcome, and so both parties are
             quits; or, there is an equal number on both sides of the
             table
             **The feast is sold/That is not often vouched, while 'tis a-making,/'Tis
             given with welcome** without the hosts frequently welcoming
             their guests, the guests may as well purchase a meal
             ceremony politeness

Y

remembrancer Lady Macbeth, who is reminding her husband of
   his duties

O proper stuff! stuff and nonsense

flaws bursts of passion

If charnel-houses and our graves must send/Those we bury, back,
   our monuments/Shall be the maws of kites if the dead return
   from where we bury them, then we will need to let birds of
   prey dispose of their bodies

Ere humane statute purged the gentle weal before good laws
   cleansed society

And all to all good wishes to everyone

speculation live, comprehending vision

If trembling I inhabit then, protest me if I tremble with fear at all,
   then call me

Augurs and understood relations prophecies and things
   connected

secret'st man of blood hidden facts of murder

at odds with disputing with, i.e. not yet neither one nor the
   other

acted ere they may be scanned be done before they're thought
   about too long

self-abuse self-delusion

initiate novice

SCENE 5   The three witches enter and meet Hecate, the goddess
of witchcraft, and their leader. She reprimands them for
not having included her in the dealings with Macbeth.
She commands them to prepare a specially strong spell
to delude Macbeth when he comes to meet them the
following morning.

COMMENT   The suggestion that Macbeth is a 'son' (line 11), albeit
'wayward', suggests that Macbeth is no longer a victim
of the witches' evil, but more an adept – one of them –
in their art. However, there can be no doubt – adept or
not – by the end of the play he has so fully embraced
evil, he has destroyed himself.

*Think about how
this scene may or
may not deepen
the tension or our
sense of the
supernatural.*

The need for 'strength' (line 28) is reflected in the
witches' offering to let Macbeth see their 'masters'
(IV.1.62).

Notice the mention of mortal's chiefest enemy (line
33) – security – the witches lull Macbeth into a false
sense of security in Act IV Scene 1.

GLOSSARY

beldams hags
Acheron river of woe, in hell

SCENE 6

*Look at the
atmosphere and
state of Scotland
as it emerges from
Lennox and the
lord's speeches.*

Lennox outlines to another lord in deeply ironic (see
Literary Terms) terms his understanding of what has
been happening in Scotland: i.e. that Macbeth is
responsible for all the murders that have plagued the
state. Malcolm is in the English court attempting to
raise military support to reclaim his throne. Macduff is
in disgrace for refusing to attend Macbeth's banquet
and is attempting to join Malcolm.

COMMENT

Macbeth earlier had said he intended to send for
Macduff (III.4.129) and this scene briefly covers the
fact that he has – Macduff has simply refused point-
blank to attend. The sense of resistance to Macbeth's
rule is now growing. From Lennox's words (and
irony), we have Macduff's refusal to comply, and
ultimately Malcolm's efforts in England to raise an
army to claim back his throne.

GLOSSARY

hit your thoughts agree with your opinions
strangely borne done in a peculiar way
pious Edward Edward the Confessor, King of England
the malevolence of fortune nothing/Takes from his high respect
  despite his loss of the throne, he is still treated with all
  honours due
that clogs me that makes my life difficult – see how Macbeth
  treats the messengers who bring bad news later in the play:
  (V.3.11) and (V.5.35)

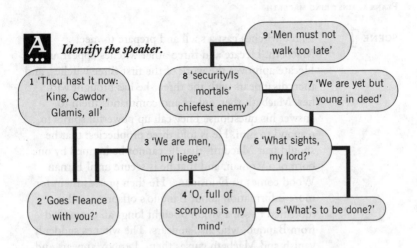

A *Identify the speaker.*

9 'Men must not walk too late'

8 'security/Is mortals' chiefest enemy'

7 'We are yet but young in deed'

1 'Thou hast it now: King, Cawdor, Glamis, all'

3 'We are men, my liege'

6 'What sights, my lord?'

2 'Goes Fleance with you?'

4 'O, full of scorpions is my mind'

5 'What's to be done?'

Identify the person 'to whom' this comment refers.

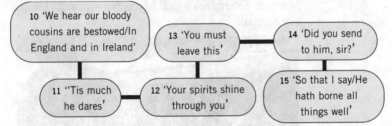

10 'We hear our bloody cousins are bestowed/In England and in Ireland'

13 'You must leave this'

14 'Did you send to him, sir?'

11 ''Tis much he dares'

12 'Your spirits shine through you'

15 'So that I say/He hath borne all things well'

Check your answers on page 92.

B *Consider these issues.*

a Whether Banquo should have revealed his suspicions concerning Macbeth.

b How Macbeth persuades the murderers to undertake his task.

c What the effect of guilt is on Macbeth.

d Whether the appearance of Banquo's ghost is real or a figment of Macbeth's guilty conscience.

e What Macbeth's guests would conclude after the banquet.

f How the relationship between Macbeth and his wife changes.

g What the reappearance of the witches suggests.

ACT IV

SCENE 1   Three witches cast a spell and prepare to meet
Macbeth. Hecate and three other witches appear and
Hecate approves the work of the first three witches, and
then disappears with the three she has brought with
her. Macbeth then enters and commands them to
answer his questions. They call up powerful spirits to
respond to him. He is told three prophecies: that he
should fear Macduff, that he cannot be harmed by one
born of a woman, and that he is secure until Birnan
Wood comes to Dunsinane. He then presses them for
more information about Banquo's offspring and is
mortified to see a vision of eight kings all descended
from Banquo, who also appears. The witches suddenly
vanish and Macbeth curses them. Lennox appears and
informs Macbeth that Macduff has fled to England.
Macbeth determines to kill Macduff's wife and children
as a reprisal.

COMMENT   The supernatural atmosphere is charged with evil. The
witches' spells are particularly nauseating in the level of
detail they depict – here, if any further proof were
needed, is evidence of precisely how unnatural these
hags are.

Prior to his arrival, Macbeth is described as 'Something
wicked' (line 45) – not even someone. Macbeth is one

of their ilk now. This is in line with the overall effect of evil in dehumanising the personality – the bestial imagery (see Literary Terms) commented upon was also a manifestation of this. So is the fact that they do a 'deed without a name' (line 48).

The only thing that matters to Macbeth now is his own position.

Earlier uncertainties have been stripped away. Before, the witches informed him of the prophecies; now he demands of them what he wants to know. He even threatens the powerful master spirits with a curse if they do not answer him (line 104). And when he leaves, there is no more agonising about what he needs to do – or discussing the situation with his wife – Macduff's castle is to be attacked. An incidental point here is the depths to which Macbeth has fallen in murdering, without any compunction, women and children.

One consequence of his visit is the certainty of 'security' (III.5.32), which has troubled Macbeth from the outset. One factor in establishing the trustworthiness of the prophecies in Macbeth's mind is the speed with which they happen: 'Cawdor' (I.3.104) followed immediately upon their pronunciation of it; now, having been told to watch out for Macduff, Lennox appears with the same warning. Of course, the irony (see Literary Terms) is that all the prophecies are double-edged and turn against him. Banquo's comment accurately reflects the truth: 'The instruments of darkness tell us truths;/Win us with honest trifles, to betray's/In deepest consequence' (I.3.123–5). These words are prophetic and an indictment of all that Macbeth comes to believe.

Two or three horsemen ride to bring Macbeth word that Macduff is fled – the spies he has 'fee'd' (III.4.131).

GLOSSARY   **brinded** streaked

Harpier name of third witches' familiar, and probably derived from harpy: a fierce and filthy monster, half bird, half woman

mummy mummified part of the body

maw and gulf of the ravined throat and stomach full with devoured prey

slips seedlings (yew believed to be poisonous)

drab prostitute

chaudron entrails

lodged laid flat

nature's germens the seeds of things, here the sense of the essences of reality

I'll make assurance double sure,/And take a bond of fate I'll make the prophecy doubly certain by killing Macduff

bodements predictions

live the lease of nature die a natural death

A show of eight kings the Stuart line of Kings of Scotland, and subsequently England and Ireland

the flighty purpose never is o'ertook/Unless the deed go with it we cannot realise our intentions unless we do them at the moment we imagine them

SCENE *2*

Is Lady Macduff right to blame Macduff of cowardice?

Lady Macduff is with her son and Ross. Ross informs her that her husband has fled to England. Lady Macduff accuses her husband of cowardice. Ross makes his excuses and leaves. The son interrogates his mother about the meaning of the word traitor. A messenger abruptly arrives, warns of danger, and leaves. Murderers enter, kill her son, and pursue her with the same purpose.

COMMENT

The scene is particularly affecting because Lady Macduff and her son are entirely innocent of any crime. At least with the murder of Banquo and the attempted murder of Fleance, Macbeth had a 'reason' for it. Here there is no such justification. It is not coincidental, though, that the desire to eliminate all unfortunates that 'trace him in his line' (IV.1.152) immediately follows Macbeth's vision of the line of Banquo as kings – clearly, the thought of dynasty obsesses and torments Macbeth. The scene is also affecting because the

Y

Undoubtedly, the murder of these two helpless innocents is not only a brutal but a cowardly act, which must reflect upon Macbeth's character as well as the murderers.

dialogue between Lady Macduff and her son reveals two delightful human beings: the waste of life that Macbeth's ambition has incurred is more fully realised in this snapshot of two good people about to be 'snuffed' out, than in all the talk about the stifling and tyrannical political atmosphere of Scotland under his reign.

We do not see Lady Macduff murdered on stage (unlike her son), but we do see and further hear her screaming 'murder' as she flees offstage. This seems a particularly brilliant piece of staging that reinforces a central thematic (see Literary Terms) idea. To have had her murdered onstage would have created a moment of fear and suspense, but which in the execution is immediately over: another dead body is on the stage. To have her fleeing offstage, screaming murder, is to prolong that sense of imminent fear and to leave it ringing in our ears – in fact, it is to leave us in uncertainty till we learn the truth in the next scene. This is a natural consequence of the kind of fear that Macbeth himself detests – not knowing, not being sure. His reign has created this unease for everybody. The insecurity and uncertainty becomes a tangible phenomenon (through the sound) for the audience watching the play.

Ross is sympathetic, but cleverly manages not to be present when the murderers arrive. Ross always seems to be on the 'right' side of things.

The discussion on traitors is highly pertinent – the real traitor, of course, is Macbeth. The discussion with her son, though, points us towards a consideration of all forms of loyalty, domestic as well as political. Although Lady Macduff berates her husband's cowardice, in front of the murderers she shows courage and defends her husband.

A small point, but these murderers, compared with
those who murdered Banquo, are far more savage and
brutal. And this too indicates the increasing
degradation of Macbeth.

GLOSSARY

The fits o' the season the unexpected happenings of this time

when we hold rumour/From what we fear when all we believe are
rumours, based on what we fear might be the truth

The net nor lime, the pitfall nor the gin all kinds of traps – ironic,
in that they are in a trap themselves

Poor birds they are not set for no traps are laid for worthless
birds – in other words, why should he worry about a trap when
he is not of any value?

wit enough for thee sensible enough for you, given your age

enow enough

Though in your state of honour I am perfect Though I fully realise
your rank

To do worse to you were fell cruelty to do more than frighten you
would be cruel

unsanctified unholy and unblessed – the suggestion being that
the mere presence of such a person defiles God's creation

shag-haired rough-haired

egg this image – an egg is an as yet unformed bird – is exactly
in line with Macbeth's central preoccupation: wiping out the
line of Macduff

SCENE 3

*How does
Shakespeare
predict what sort
of King Malcolm
will make?
Describe how you
think he will
behave once he
regains his throne.*

In England Malcolm entertains Macduff: he is testing
his integrity because – with all the spies and traitors
that Macbeth has created – he is fearful he might be on
Macbeth's side. Malcolm pretends that he is even more
depraved than Macbeth, and so should not ascend the
throne. Macduff's lament for Scotland, however,
convinces Malcolm – who then retracts his confessions
of evil – that Macduff is sincere and opposed to
Macbeth. He reveals to Macduff that he has English
support for an invasion of Scotland. Macduff is
confused but pleased by this turn of events. A doctor

appears and mentions the saintly work of King Edward the Confessor. After he leaves, Malcolm and Macduff discuss the true virtues of kingship, and how this is transmitted to succeeding monarchs. Ross arrives with news and eventually, reluctantly, informs Macduff that his family has been murdered. Macduff is temporarily overwhelmed by the news, but collects himself. He is resolved to support Malcolm and vows to kill Macbeth himself.

COMMENT

The integrity of Macduff is clearly shown in his refusal to accept Malcolm's account of himself – 'Fit to govern!/No, not to live!'

This scene provides a balance to the others in Act IV. The evil of Macbeth's visit to the witches, and the dreadful murder of the Macduffs, now gives way to more 'normal' emotions and reactions. Malcolm is suspicious of Macduff – neither of them at the beginning of the scene know what Macbeth has done to Macduff's family. One cause of Malcolm's suspicion is, as he says, 'He hath not touched you yet' (line 14), meaning that Macbeth has not injured Macduff's family (a dramatic irony – see Literary Terms – in the circumstances of the preceding scene), and so why should Macduff quarrel with Macbeth? Malcolm has already experienced traitors who have tried to entrap him (lines 117–20), and so is wary of committing himself.

The scene, although full of dramatic tension as Malcolm plays his game with Macduff, and as Ross enters, reluctant to reveal the truth, is largely static: it concludes with the action they are going to take. So it is important as a springboard into Act V. But equally, it is important in the number of dramatic contrasts it provides. Of fundamental importance is the contrast between King Macbeth and King Edward. Also, we should bear in mind here that Malcolm will be king – and we see the kind of man he is, the values he possesses, and there is another reference to remind us how good Duncan was. This scene, therefore, does explore the issues of kingship. Further, there are other personal contrasts that should be noted: Macduff's reaction to the death of his wife might usefully be compared with Macbeth's reaction (V.5.17-27). Such a contrast will show how desensitised Macbeth has become to all normal human feeling. Finally, in trying to understand human character, we might want to ask why Ross, in relating the death of Macduff's family, omitted to mention his own presence and conversation with Lady Macduff and his 'cousin' (IV.2.25) shortly before?

The reference to the way a monarch might cure the king's Evil (Scrofula) with a touch and how this gift is passed on was surely present not only to contrast with Macbeth's cursed reign, but also to gratify King James, who saw himself as having this gift.

GLOSSARY

Bestride our down-fallen birthdom fight for our native land

Like syllable of dolour the same cry of grief

sole mere

You may deserve of him Macbeth may reward you (for betraying me)

the brightest Satan himself, sometimes called Lucifer: angel of light

rawness unprotected state – Malcolm suspects Macduff of treachery because he left his family unprotected; if he were in league with Macbeth, then this would not cause him a 'problem'

Lay thou thy basis sure establish yourself completely

affeered legally confirmed

confineless unbounded

the cistern of my lust my sexual appetite

all continent impediments would o'erbear all proper limits would be removed

convey indulge secretly

y

to greatness dedicate themselves be sexually available to you (ironically – see Literary Terms – spoken)

summer-seeming lust lust is a product of youth; whereas avarice is perennial

the sword of the reason for taking arms against

Died every day she lived died in the Christian sense of mortifying the self through discipline and prayer

the chance of goodness/Be like our warranted quarrel may the chance of winning be in proportion to the justice of our cause

Their malady convinces/The great assay of art their illness defeats all medical skill

a golden stamp a gold coin

nothing/But who knows nothing only someone wholly ignorant

A modern ecstasy a commonplace emotion

flowers in their caps sprigs of heather in a highlander's bonnet

fee-grief grief for one particular person

Ne'er pull your hat upon your brows don't bottle up or hide your grief

hell-kite bird of prey – here meaning Macbeth

Naught worthless

Our lack is nothing but our leave all we need to do is to take our leave of the King

TEST YOURSELF (Act IV)

A Identify the speaker.

1 'Say if thou'dst rather hear it from our mouths/Or from our masters'

2 'No boasting like a fool'

3 'He loves us not'

4 'I am not treacherous'

5 'But I have none./The king-becoming graces'

6 'They were all struck for thee'

7 'Macbeth is ripe for shaking'

Identify the person 'to whom' this comment refers.

8 'O well done! I commend your pains'

9 'His flight was madness'

10 'Why in that rawness left you wife and child'

11 'If such a one be fit to govern, speak'

12 'Such sanctity hath heaven given his hand'

Check your answers on page 92.

B Consider these issues.

a How Macbeth reacts to the witches and their prophecies.

b How the prophecies link to future occurrences.

c Whether you feel most pity for Macduff or for his family and which details help build our sense of pity for both of them.

d Why and how Malcolm is compelled to test Macduff.

e What contrasts exist between the courts of England and Scotland.

ACT V

SCENE 1

In Macbeth's castle at Dunsinane a doctor and a waiting-gentlewoman discuss their patient, Lady Macbeth. The gentlewoman refuses to discuss what she has heard Lady Macbeth say in her sleep, since she has no witness to corroborate her statements. As the doctor attempts to persuade her, Lady Macbeth appears, sleepwalking. They both hear her reveal her guilt and watch her as she futilely attempts to remove the blood from her hands. The doctor concludes that she is more in need of spiritual rather than medical attention.

COMMENT

The clear mental breakdown of Lady Macbeth is both deeply affecting and also strikes the audience, in psychological terms, as profoundly true. There are a number of points to notice. First, as with all guilt, there is the obsession with the past. Remember, it was Lady Macbeth who said, 'what's done is done' (III.2.12), thus suggesting that it would no longer be of concern. Here, despite all her courage and ambition and strength of purpose, all that has been 'done' is not past, but present – and ever present – in her mind. She herself refers to her own earlier declaration when she says, 'What's done cannot be undone' (lines 62–3). The contrast with Macbeth himself could not be more marked – 'I cannot taint with fear' (V.3.3). Until the prophecies start unravelling, Macbeth seems impervious to concern.

Who do you think is the stronger character – Lady Macbeth, or her husband?

Secondly, there is deep dramatic irony (see Literary Terms) in the fact that physical symptoms of her guilt include the forlorn hope of washing clean her hands. We need to link this to both her statement that 'a little water clears us of this deed' (II.2.67) and Macbeth's insight upon actually committing the murder that 'Will all great Neptune's ocean wash this blood/Clean from my hand? No' (II.2.60–1). Although they share a common aim (to gain the throne), their beliefs are different: ultimately, however, all their beliefs are proved hollow.

Finally, it is worth noting that most of the play is written in blank verse (see Literary Terms). Notable exceptions are the Porter's scene (II.3) and this appearance of Lady Macbeth. Before, and particularly in the first two Acts, Lady Macbeth's speech had been blazing and fiery blank verse – the strong rhythms reflecting her strong grasp on reality, and her determination. Now, she speaks in prose (see Literary Terms) – choppy, abrupt, lurching from one incident to another, and even descending to doggerel (see Literary Terms) with the rhyme of Fife and wife (line 41). Shakespeare's writing here is brilliantly recreating what it means to 'breakdown' – the language is 'breaking' down under the strain she is under. It is therefore not surprising that she commits suicide – she can no longer hold 'it' together, and on death, of course, language disappears altogether. Note the contrast between the English court where the King heals 'Evil', and here where the disease is beyond any physician's competence.

GLOSSARY
into the field into the battlefield – perhaps no coincidence in the timing, as physical retribution draws closer, this may have triggered Lady Macbeth's final crisis
perturbation in nature mental disorder
mated bewildered

SCENE 2   Knowing that Malcolm is marching north with a troop of English soldiers, we are introduced to the rebel Scottish powers who are determined to overthrow Macbeth. They plan to meet up with the English at Birnan Wood. The Thanes comment on how uneasy Macbeth must now feel, as his inadequacies and guilt must face the test – and they are confident of victory.

COMMENT   From the imminence of action at the close of Act IV, we now find the hurly-burly of war – plans, preparations and advances. The scene also serves, in its reference to Birnan Wood and Dunsinane, to remind us of the prophecies, and so tantalise us: how can Macbeth be defeated if the witches are always right in their predictions? This scene, then, helps accelerate the build-up – we are anxious for the climax.

The fact that the recovery of the crown by Malcolm is not solely through English forces is also important (bearing in mind that James the First was an audience for the play). Scotland, too, played an important role in casting off its tyrannical yoke.

Notice the imagery (see Literary Terms) of clothing surfacing once more (lines 20–2) – Macbeth is simply not big enough to hold onto the crown.

GLOSSARY   **dear causes** heartfelt wrongs (and so grounds for action)
mortified dead (in other words, a dead man could feel the
   wrongs done to Malcolm and Macduff)
He cannot buckle his distempered cause/Within the belt of rule he
   cannot satisfactorily control his forces
Now minutely revolts upbraid his faith-breach now very frequent
   rebellions expose his own treachery
pestered senses harrowed nerves
the medicine Malcolm

SCENE 3   Macbeth enters with the doctor and attendants. He is in robust and fearless mood: the prophecies give him complete confidence that he is unassailable. A servant is abused as he reports that the English troops are arriving. Macbeth orders his armour and asks the doctor to cure his wife. He curtly dismisses the doctor's medical advice and enquires of him, what would cure his country. But is scarcely listening to the doctor's reply – his mind is obsessed with the prophecies, which alone guarantee his security.

COMMENT   That Macbeth is doomed should be obvious from this scene alone: the dependence he now has on the prophecies is paralysing his own decision-making and

ACTION AGAINST KING MACBETH

Compare Macbeth's preparation for war with that of the Thanes in Scene 2?

capacity for action. 'Bring me no more reports' (line 1) is a desperate statement for someone engaged in a war to utter – intelligence gathering is of primary importance. He begins and ends the scene reciting the prophecies – they have become a mantra to him. On them and them alone his survival depends.

The presence of the doctor again from Act V Scene 1 provides a neat sense of continuity and also of dramatic irony (see Literary Terms): the question of ministering to Lady Macbeth extends to the wider issue of ministering to the country, which has, as Macbeth notes, a 'disease' (line 51). The political aspect of treachery is never very far away. Also, the comments on Lady Macbeth's health, mostly made by Macbeth to the doctor, apply equally to Macbeth himself. But he, of course, will have 'none of it' (line 48). Instead his restless energy seeks violent outlet – the casual way he orders the hanging of anyone talking of fear (line 36) shows how callous and depraved he has become. Yet despite that, there is a part of him which still evokes compassion: his recognition of the life he might have had – which included honour, love and troops of friends (lines 24–5) – cannot but touch the heart. He knows, and relishes, what is good – but has chosen the opposite. This is his tragedy (see Literary Terms).

GLOSSARY

sway rule myself

over-red make red (because by pricking it the blood will cover your cowardly white)

dis-seat overthrow

mouth-honour lip service

thick-coming fancies frequently appearing hallucinations

cast/The water inspect the urine (to diagnose what is wrong)

rhubarb, senna all natural substances thought to have healing properties

Y

SCENE 4

Look for evidence which shows that Malcolm is young and inexperienced?

Malcolm orders each of his men to cut down a bough from Birnan Wood and to carry it in front of them as they march in order to conceal their numbers from Macbeth. They learn that Macbeth intends to remain in Dunsinane – his strategy being to endure a siege. This is his only hope, since his troops are demoralised and fight for him out of necessity, not commitment.

COMMENT

A neat pattern emerges, which simply and effectively increases tension. Scene 1 led us into the diseased mind of Lady Macbeth; in Scene 2 we switched to the preparation of the Scottish Thanes who were planning to attack Macbeth. Scene 3 returned us to the castle. This time we witnessed Macbeth's diseased mind, but were also made much more aware of Scotland's disease. Now, in Scene 4, we alternate back to the cure for all these diseases: the English army led by Malcolm, the rightful king. As Seyward concludes: 'certain issues strokes must arbitrate' (line 20) – a bloody operation to remove the disease by lopping it off. We have seen, therefore, the situation in both camps – and we note the contrasts – now the battle must commence.

Again we are reminded of prophecy in the reference to the Wood. The witches only appear in four scenes (and two of these extremely briefly), but their influence pervades the whole play.

GLOSSARY

Our setting down before't our laying siege to his castle
advantage to be given opportunity to be taken
Both more and less both great men and men of lesser importance
Let out just censures/Attend the true event if our judgements are to be right, then we must see how events unfold (i.e. not to be too confident beforehand)
Thoughts speculative their unsure hopes relate speculations are really uncertain

ACTION AGAINST KING MACBETH

SCENE 5

Compare
Macbeth's reaction
to Seyton's
announcement
with his reaction
to the messenger
following.

Macbeth enters boasting his castle can easily endure a siege: he is confident of victory. He regrets that he cannot go out to face the traitors – too many have defected from his banner. A woman's scream is heard and Seyton goes to investigate. Macbeth reflects that nothing terrifies him now. Seyton returns and informs Macbeth his wife has died. For him this is a confirmation that life is meaningless. A messenger arrives and informs him that Birnan Wood indeed moves towards Dunsinane Castle. Outraged, and in some considerable doubt about his destiny and the meaning of the prophecies, he immediately changes his strategy and orders an attack.

COMMENT

The confidence of Macbeth in his strategy – bolstered by the witches' prophecy – is in marked contrast to the humility present in Malcolm's camp.

Lady Macbeth's death was inevitable from all the comments made in Act V. But there was no point in showing it on stage – it is much more effective (and neatly symmetrical when we consider Lady Macduff's end) to hear her final scream. The interest of her death is in Macbeth's reaction to it. This can be read in a number of ways. Is he entirely indifferent and emotionless – 'signifying nothing' (line 28)? Does his soliloquy (see Literary Terms) suggest mere cynicism as a last response – 'Told by an idiot' (line 27)? Or does the word 'hereafter' (line 17) signify his realisation of the real loss in his life? Whichever might be true, and they are not exclusive, there is something in this isolation that he is suffering that cannot help but move us to pity him, despite our revulsion for all that Macbeth stands for.

Ironically, it is his obsessive and literal belief in the prophecies that destroys him. Now believing the Wood to be moving, he succumbs to a fatalistic mentality and abandons his strategy – and the high security of the castle that would 'laugh a siege to scorn' (line 3). By foolishly doing so, despite the fact that on his own admission he has not enough troops to win, he ensures the prophecy comes true. Of course, this ignores one other fact about his state of mind: 'I 'gin to be aweary of the sun' (line 49) – he no longer cares whether he lives or dies.

GLOSSARY
dareful bravely
fell of hair skin with the hair on
petty pace small, trivial step
cling wither
I pull in resolution my confidence falters
equivocation double meaning (and sense of doublecross)
avouches asserts
estate o'the world God's creation

SCENE 6

Malcolm, Macduff and Seyward with their army under camouflage approach Macbeth's castle. Battle commences. Macbeth is trapped but unbeaten. He encounters Young Seyward and kills him in combat.

Meanwhile, Macduff seeks out Macbeth alone. Macbeth's army capitulates and Seyward invites Malcolm to take the castle. Macbeth sees the day is lost

ACTION AGAINST KING MACBETH

Earlier Macbeth but will not contemplate suicide. At this point he
had said he could encounters Macduff. Initially, he refuses to fight
not taint with fear. Macduff, but Macduff insists. As they fight Macbeth
Macduff's mocks Macduff – no man born of a woman can defeat
revelation him. However, his confidence entirely evaporates when
concerning his birth Macduff informs him that he was not 'born', but
is a dramatically delivered through a Caesarean operation. Macbeth is
charged moment. It suddenly afraid and refuses to fight. He realises how
is, perhaps, not profoundly the prophecies have betrayed him. Macduff
unconnected that as now baits Macbeth. In a final act of courage Macbeth
Macbeth experiences fights Macduff and is slain. The battle has been won by
a real human Malcolm and he now is anxious to account for all his
emotion, his courage friends. Seyward – through Ross – discovers his son is
too returns in the dead. As they commiserate on this, Macduff arrives
wake of it. with the decapitated head of Macbeth, and hails
Malcolm King of Scotland. Malcolm gives thanks by
promoting the thanes to new-formed earls. He intends
to put right the evil caused by Macbeth and invites
everyone to his coronation at Scone.

COMMENT This scene is, in some editions of the play, divided up
into four separate scenes. For the purposes of this study,
this is not important.

Young Seyward is not a significant character in the
play, but his killing by Macbeth is symptomatic of all
the promise that Macbeth has blighted by his reign and
activities. It also reminds us that Macbeth is, perhaps
first and foremost, a warrior. The play establishes early
on his ferocious credentials as a fighter – if we have
forgotten about this, because subsequently Macbeth
operates through murderers, then in this final scene we
are reminded of where his true strength is. This is
important – otherwise Macduff's achievement in slaying
him in one-to-one combat is diminished. We might
like to discuss, however, whether Macbeth's initial
reason for not wanting to fight with Macduff – 'my soul
is too much charged' (line 44) – is his genuine reason,

Y

or is it his memory of the witches' prophecy: 'beware Macduff' (IV.1.70)?

The fact that Macbeth is primarily a warrior is also important in our final evaluation of him: through succumbing to the temptation that the witches afforded him, the witches succeeded in destroying almost every aspect of his true humanity. Even his courage temporarily deserts him (line 61) when he learns from Macduff how false the prophecies are – yet his courage returns: he will not yield. He will, as it were, take on Fate as well as Macduff – 'Yet I will try the last' (line 71) – and this, while it does not mitigate his crimes, does enable us to see some remnant of his great bravery.

The betrayal by the witches is doubly gross in that they refer to Macbeth as a wayward son – that is , one of their own kind.

Macbeth's analysis of the witches' – 'these juggling fiends' (line 58) – prophecies comes full circle: he was warned by Banquo (I.3.121–5) and now he has experienced and knows exactly what Banquo predicted. Further, juggling in a 'double sense' (line 59) ties in with the idea of equivocation running through the play. Equivocation, of course, particularly given its contemporary relevance to the Gunpowder Plot is synonymous with treason. Ironically (see Literary Terms), just as Macbeth betrayed Duncan, so the witches have betrayed Macbeth. When deliberating the pros and cons of treason and murder Macbeth commented 'we but teach/Bloody instructions, which, being taught, return/To plague the inventor' (I.7.8–10). This, too, has come true – he has had no rest as his own men and thanes have constantly defected from his cause, and of course his ultimate trust in the witches also proves misplaced.

The imagery (see Literary Terms) and use of children runs through this play and adds a particular pathos (see Literary Terms) to various scenes. Suffice to note here: it is the *Caesar*ean born Macduff who defeats Macbeth.

Earlier, Macbeth had commented on feeling like Mark Antony before *Caesar* (III.1.56) when near Banquo. Clearly, Macduff is the man of destiny born, as it were, to destroy Macbeth.

Do you think the ending is satisfying? Will Malcolm make a good King?

The crowning of Malcolm concludes the play, but one important prophecy is still unfulfilled: that Banquo's issue will attain the throne. This means that the ending of the play can be interpreted in two quite different ways. First, a joyous occasion on which the innocent and honest Malcolm will make good all the wrongs during his reign. Second, a view of some productions that see the evil commenced by the witches as so endemic that another alternative is possible: namely, a cold and calculating King Malcolm surveys his victory – seeing Fleance in his army (not authorised by the text) – and realises that he must assassinate Fleance if he is to remain King.

GLOSSARY

undeeded unused

strike beside us either, fight by our side, or deliberately aim to miss us

play the Roman fool as Mark Antony did, committing suicide to avoid capture by Caesar

terms can give thee out words can speak about you

palter with equivocate or deceive

Some must go off some must die

Had he his hurts before? Was he wounded on the front? (facing the enemy, not running away)

thy kingdom's pearl the nobles of Scotland

Producing forth the cruel ministers/Of this dead butcher capturing the wicked men who carried out Macbeth's orders

Y

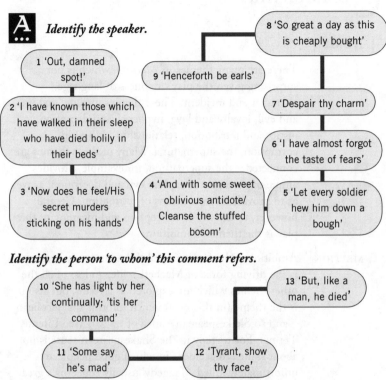

A *Identify the speaker.*

8 'So great a day as this is cheaply bought'

1 'Out, damned spot!'

9 'Henceforth be earls'

2 'I have known those which have walked in their sleep who have died holily in their beds'

7 'Despair thy charm'

6 'I have almost forgot the taste of fears'

3 'Now does he feel/His secret murders sticking on his hands'

4 'And with some sweet oblivious antidote/ Cleanse the stuffed bosom'

5 'Let every soldier hew him down a bough'

Identify the person 'to whom' this comment refers.

10 'She has light by her continually; 'tis her command'

13 'But, like a man, he died'

11 'Some say he's mad'

12 'Tyrant, show thy face'

Check your answers on page 92.

B *Consider these issues.*

a The change in Lady Macbeth's character and fortune, and the reasons for it.

b How Macbeth increasingly loses control of the situation – and of his troops – through the final act.

c Whether there is anything we can admire in Macbeth by the end of the play and how we might sum up his character.

d What role the supernatural has played in the destruction of Macbeth and whether the witches did tell him the 'truth'.

e How Shakespeare creates a sense of action and purposefulness throughout the act.

f The future of Scotland under Malcolm and the role of Fleance.

PART THREE

COMMENTARY

THEMES

There are many themes in *Macbeth*, which is not surprising given the play's richness of language, character and incident. These themes include: goodness and evil, loyalty and love, hypocrisy and deception, justice and retribution, relationships, kingship, corruption, the supernatural. Many of these themes are connected – the supernatural, for example, provides ample opportunity to explore evil and deception, as well as to provide its own means of retribution. Central, however, to the whole conception and meaning of the play is the theme of ambition.

AMBITION   Ambition is the fundamental theme not only because it is the driving force of Macbeth's life, and so of all the other themes which are explored as a result, but also it is the theme (in this play) which informs the 'Jacobean' – and so Shakespearean – idea of tragedy (see Literary Terms). For tragedy in the Shakespearean sense is not about some sad accident in which good people are unfortunately killed. 'Tragedy' usually concerns a great person – the hero – who through some weakness of character falls from grace, endures intense sufferings (which fascinate the audience), and who inevitably dies. In fact, who must die as a consequence of their weakness. Thus, if we look at 'The Tragedy of Macbeth', we find all these ingredients. And if we consider what is the hero's weakness, it must and can only be ambition.

Macbeth says this specifically when he is attempting to resist the murder of Duncan: 'I have no spur ... but only/Vaulting ambition which o'erleaps itself' (I.7.25–7). This acknowledgement comes after he has considered all the good reasons for not murdering

Duncan – only ambition is left to overrule his troubled conscience. Furthermore, whilst the influence of both Lady Macbeth and the witches is strong, their power over Macbeth is only possible because the ambition is already there. We see this with Lady Macbeth when she derides his intention to 'proceed no further in this business' (I.7.31). Her comment 'Was the hope drunk/Wherein you dressed yourself?' (I.7.35-6) clearly implies that he has raised her expectations of the throne – she did not have to raise the issue with him. And so too with the witches. Their intention is to meet with Macbeth (I.1.7), not Banquo. Banquo they know is incorruptible. On first meeting Macbeth we find him starting and seeming to fear something which sounds 'so fair' (I.3.51) and this can only be because his ambition has caused him already to entertain treasonous thoughts. Macbeth, then, is a hero but one who is fatally undermined by his ambition; and the consequences of such ambition – also explored through his wife who is similarly inclined – are the fabric of the play. Put another way: it is his ambition that leads the witches to Macbeth, and it is ambition which leads Macbeth to murder, treason, hypocrisy, corruption and deepest evil.

THE SUPERNATURAL

The supernatural, and witchcraft in particular, are also thematically important. Certainly, they are a major contributory factor to the play's enduring popularity. The presence of the supernatural in the play raises all sorts of questions concerning reality and appearances. Do witches really exist and have such powers? Or, more precisely, did Shakespeare believe in them? Further, assuming they did appear, was the dagger (II.1) that led Macbeth on visible or an hallucination? And what about Banquo's ghost (III.4)? And Lady Macbeth's spot (V.1)? This last question indicates an area where the supernatural shades into the psychological, and there is much appreciative comment on how accurate Shakespeare's understanding of a guilt-laden conscience might be, although he was writing some three hundred or so years before psychology became a science.

Two points are vital. The first is to realise that in Shakespeare's time witchcraft was a substantial issue: James the First believed in witchcraft. People generally believed in it, and it was a capital offence to be a witch, because they were considered enemies to society. Thus, the witches are real, and any attempt to present the play purely in psychological terms does not match Shakespeare's conception.

The play Macbeth *is steeped in Christian cosmology; the evil of the world is horribly real but ultimately self-defeating.*

This is important if we consider, for example, the invocation of Lady Macbeth to the dark forces (I.5.36–52): she is, in this scene, quite literally asking demonic spirits to possess her mind and body so that all human pity can be excised. To remove the supernatural aspect of this 'possession' is fundamentally to weaken both its dramatic impact and its grip on her being. The actress Sarah Siddons, generally considered one of the greatest Lady Macbeths, observed of the character that 'having impiously delivered herself up to the excitements of hell … [Lady Macbeth] is abandoned to the guidance of the demons she has invoked'. In short, 'naturalistic' interpretations fall short in their depiction.

Secondly, the supernatural is present in the play not *only* as an embodiment of evil. True, it is the witches we remember and their prophecies, because they are so dramatic. But set against these, there are references to prayer (II.2.24), sanctity (IV.3.109), cleansing (V.2.28) and even another sort of prophecy (IV.3.157). On this latter point it is worth bearing in mind that not only the witches' predictions come true: Duncan says, 'But signs of nobleness, like stars, shall shine/On all

deservers' (I.4.42–3) and this occurs when Malcolm
elevates the thanes to earls in the final speech of the
play (V.6.101–3). But the most important aspect of
insisting that there are two sides to the supernatural
theme returns us to the play's focus and hero: Macbeth.

The supernatural backdrop to the play intensifies our
sense of evil, surely; but it does not dictate events.
Macbeth is a free agent and has freewill. There is no
tragedy (see Literary Terms) at all without the
realisation that Macbeth has chosen his course of
action, and each subsequent action is a reaffirmation of
that original, and bad, choice. It is not without
significance that the doctor's diagnosis of Lady
Macbeth (applicable to Macbeth himself) talks of the
need for a 'divine' (V.1.70). Even at this stage,
confession and repentance are possible – although, as
we know, not chosen. When the doctor mentions the
requirement for the patient to 'minister to himself'
(V.3.46), suggesting a need for self-examination,
Macbeth's retort is unambiguous: 'I'll none of it'
(V.3.47). One consequence of this, therefore, is that on
the one hand, the supernatural is less important,
perhaps, than its dramatic impact portends; but on the
other hand, whilst mankind is free to make decisions,
the presence of the supernatural does invoke a cosmic
dimension and importance to all such decisions – this
means damnation has a fearful reality about it. And, as
we read or see the play, who cannot but think Macbeth
is just such a one as has chosen damnation?

*Without freewill,
of course, there
would be no
damnation and no
tragedy. It is
because Macbeth
'chooses' that he
must suffer the
consequences of his
choices.*

STRUCTURE

Macbeth is Shakespeare's shortest tragedy (see Literary
Terms). One reason for this is that there is no subplot.
All the action contributes to the central focus on
Macbeth himself. This creates – as befits the intensity

of evil in the play – a unified and powerful effect. The play itself comprises the traditional five acts, which are then subdivided into scenes, but within that framework the structure is two-fold: we see the rise of Macbeth to power, and we see the fall. Both activities are prefaced by the witches' contributions. The turning point is in Act III at the banquet scene. Here Macbeth has achieved the full limit and splendour of the power he has and is ever going to achieve: at this point, Macduff excepted, the Thanes of Scotland are disposed to accept him. But the murder of Banquo produces catastrophic consequences, including the immediate usurpation of his chair by the ghost. It is following this event that Macbeth decides to revisit the witches, and from here onwards his decline in actual power – although not in depravity, which increases – begins.

The two-fold structure does not imply good and evil are two 'equal' opposites. That would be a delusion that evil itself would want. Rather, the play sees evil as unnatural – a disease – a parasitic and microscopic entity in reality – which attacks the healthy 'body'. 'Body' here is both the individual and the state.

This two-fold structure can be viewed in a number of other ways. It reflects the idea of crime and consequence: Macbeth himself comments on the dangers of 'even-handed justice' (I.7.10) and this proves true in terms of the play's structure: what he does in the first half of the play, returns to haunt him in the second half. Equally, we see how the characters of Macbeth and Lady Macbeth pivot round the two-fold structure: it is Lady Macbeth who exults in evil till the middle point of the play, and her husband who is fearful of the damnable consequences; after the assassination of Banquo these positions are reversed.

This point about a two-fold structure should not surprise us when we reflect upon the elemental nature of the play: it is about good versus evil, and foul being fair (I.1.9). These oppositions and contrasts run through the whole play.

There are many clues as to what a character is like in any work of fiction, but three questions are central to any full answer. What does the character do? What does the character say (and/or think)? What do other characters say about that character? If we bear these questions in mind when looking at the major and minor characters in *Macbeth*, we should form an accurate estimate of their qualities.

MACBETH

Ambitious
Brave
Treacherous
Murderous
Imaginative
Hypocritical

Macbeth is a man of action: the play concerns the things he does. He is a fearless warrior – and an important lord – who defends his king against treachery. However, ambition is his fatal weakness. He allows, first the witches' prophecy and then his wife's ambition for him, to undermine his integrity. It is clear that he is not easily won over to evil – his conscience is strong, and throws up many objections to his doing the deed. However, he is also too easily influenced in the direction that he secretly desires to go. Once he has decided, he does not deviate, and each step subsequently reaffirms his initial choice. Macbeth, then, is determined, and with his determination goes a violent and ruthless nature.

One problem for him is that he has, initially at least, a conscience and a highly developed imaginative faculty – he sees all too well in his mind the horrors of what he is proposing to do – but he shuts out the implications of what this is telling him. He destroys his finer thoughts and feelings in his ascent to the throne. Many of these more sensitive aspects of his character are revealed through soliloquys (see Literary Terms). This leads to our view of him as a hypocrite: in public he behaves one way, but in private – on his own, with Lady Macbeth or with the witches – he behaves very differently. It also leads to his moments of weakness – before and after murdering Duncan, in seeing Banquo's ghost – when the strength of his 'realisation' threatens to 'unman'

(III.4.72) him. The question of manhood is important in understanding the character of Macbeth. It is an appeal to his manhood that is Lady Macbeth's strategy in persuading him to murder Duncan in the first place; she also makes a similar appeal during the banquet scene. We also notice that Macbeth himself appeals to the murderers of Banquo in terms of whether they are manly enough to do the deed. And it is Macduff's final taunt that stirs Macbeth to fight to the death. Therefore, we can say that there is in Macbeth's character a profound need to prove himself, which he identifies with being 'manly'. Physically, Macbeth is strong; emotionally and spiritually he proves weak and corruptible. Ironically (see Literary Terms), by being corrupted, even Macbeth's courage is compromised – we see this not only in the final scene with Macduff, but at the moment when he succumbs to murdering Duncan. This was not only a treacherous act, but also a cowardly one.

The witches are evil; God is good; Macbeth is human, and so a mixture of good and evil. This is what interests us about him.

This point about his manly nature is augmented by the comments made by Lady Macbeth. She thinks him 'too full o'the milk of human-kindness' (I.5.15) – an extraordinary statement in the light of the murders Macbeth commits. But we must remember: Macbeth develops and changes. When the play starts he is a god-like hero – a firm, strong, loyal character. But through allowing his ambition to suppress his good qualities, he becomes 'this tyrant' (IV.3.12 – Malcolm), this 'dwarfish thief' (V.2.22 – Angus) and this 'hellhound' (V.6.42 – Macduff). The character of Macbeth is a study of how one person can degenerate from 'Bellona's bridegroom' (I.2.55) to 'this dead butcher' (V.6.108).

Notice the scale of human achievement from the 'Bellona's bridegroom' to 'dead butcher'. Shakespearean tragedy is not about the ordinary and domestic range of emotions and actions – it concerns the great and the extreme.

LADY MACBETH

Dominant
Practical
Cunning
Determined
Dependant
Haunted

It might well be asked – so strong is the impression made by Lady Macbeth's character – why the play is not called the 'Tragedy of the Macbeths'? The reason is, possibly, that in her role she is not the coequal of Macbeth in the way that, say, Cleopatra is of Antony in Shakespeare's *Antony and Cleopatra*. Her role is vital but also supplementary to the work of the witches: Macbeth is tempted to do evil and Lady Macbeth is the key human agent – the one Macbeth trusts and loves – who ensures his temptation is thorough and complete. Despite her initial overpowering presence, she is not, of course, a hero(ine) herself. This is clearly shown by the way in which she collapses once Macbeth withdraws his confidence from her: she wants to support her husband, but she has no further role to play in his life. Thus, she withers on the sidelines and breaks down.

Lady Macbeth, when we first encounter her, is dominant, determined, powerful, and even perhaps frightening in the intensity of her uncompromising desire for her husband to ascend the throne. We understand that Macbeth has 'deep desires', but this seems tame compared with Lady Macbeth's unquenchable aspirations: within 40 lines of meeting her she is not encountering the supernatural on a journey home, rather she is summoning them into her body and soul! There is, then, a peculiarly imperious quality about her character. Further, we see in her actions – until her illness – a cool, self-possession. When Macbeth falters, she is there – and has the courage – to return the daggers, to faint at the news (and so distract attention from her husband), to dismiss the banquet.

The cast of her mind is practical – she plans the details of the murder – she has the future worked out. She is preeminently cunning. And it is she who has no truck with 'paintings' (III.4.60) of fear and supernatural solicitations: the dead are dead and cannot haunt the living. That is why she can say, 'a little water clears us of this deed' (II.2.67), because there is nothing to fear from God and old-fashioned ideas of retribution. This is also why she can happily envisage hypocrisy and falsehood. Her advice (I.5.60–74) on the subjects, Macbeth takes to heart and later returns to her as if it were his own advice (III.2.29-34).

Lady Macbeth says she knows how tender it is to love the babe that milks her (I.7.5). This suggests she has had children. How many, we do not know. Or even whether any are living. Macbeth's obsession with his own succession suggests they are. Duncan, Banquo and Macduff all display affection for their children. We do not see this from the Macbeths.

However, like Macbeth, Lady Macbeth shows moments of humanity – she would have killed Duncan herself only he reminded her of her own father. It is these small details which perhaps indicate that she is not as cold and inhuman as she affects. And this of course makes her breakdown seem the more inevitable. Ultimately, water will not wash away the stain of blood. It is ironical (see Literary Terms) that Macduff on first meeting Lady Macbeth refers to her as a 'gentle lady' (II.3.80) and one too sensitive to even hear the word 'murder' – by the end of the play she is recognised for what she is, a 'fiend-like queen' (V.6.108).

Finally, it is important to note that Shakespeare seems to draw the characters of Macbeth and Lady Macbeth very much as a linked and complementary pair: when Macbeth is weak and vacillating, Lady Macbeth is strong and vibrant; when Macbeth is callous and determined, she is tormented and disintegrating. Their fates are inextricably joined, but her role and character support Macbeth's destiny; Macbeth, in the final analysis, is too preoccupied with his own role to give support to her.

DUNCAN

Although he disappears at the end of Act I, Duncan is a major character. This is because his influence pervades the play, and in any case he sets the standard for what a King should be. Macbeth in comparison

Kind
Generous
Statesmanlike
Regal
Honest
Trusting
Honourable

with Duncan falls so far short, although ironically Macbeth aspires to be a King like Duncan, for he admires him. Even after he has murdered him, Macbeth refers to Duncan as 'gracious' (III.1.65). And when Macduff argues with Malcolm, he appeals to the fact that his father 'was a most sainted king' (IV.3.109). Therefore, the view of Duncan is consistent throughout the play (unlike views of the Macbeths) – all attest to his worth and merits.

Duncan is open, honest and sincere and perhaps the key word is honourable. He himself uses the word several times: first he uses it to describe the captain (I.2.45) who has been wounded fighting for him – it suggests a combination of courage, loyalty and integrity. Treachery is the opposite of this. The openness and sincerity is shown in the free and frank way he praises 'all deservers' (I.4.43) and rewards them appropriately too. There is a warmth about Duncan – he seems to enjoy the achievements of others and his gifts are not given to gain his own advantage. It is awful to reflect that our final view of Duncan is his kissing (I.6) his hostess, Lady Macbeth, to whom we subsequently learn he has sent a diamond by way of a present (II.1).

He seems decisive as a King, and clearly inspires loyalty in his thanes. If he has a weakness it is a consequence of his goodness – his trust. He comments himself that it is impossible to see the mind's construction in the face (I.4.12-14), but this recognition does not cause him to behave, perhaps, with a little more circumspection: trusting Macbeth, he too readily steps into his castle without appropriate safeguards.

BANQUO

Brave
Loyal
Honourable
Wise
Perceptive
Sensitive

Banquo is an important character because he begins his place in the story running parallel with Macbeth: they are both worthy thanes, both great warriors, both loyal to the king. Most importantly, they both encounter the witches and their prophecies. It is the reaction to, and subsequent development of, these prophecies which provides the starkest contrasts between Macbeth and Banquo, and which is thematically essential to the exploration of the whole idea of evil, temptation, corruption and freewill.

Banquo is courageous and loyal. And he possesses a wisdom and judgement borne out by events and acknowledged even by Macbeth, 'And to that dauntless temper of his mind/He hath a wisdom that doth guide his valour/To act in safety' (III.1.51–3). He notes Macbeth's reaction to the prophecies, spotting the 'fear'. He commands the witches to address him. Importantly, he sees precisely how dangerous such prophecies might be: how they might 'win us to our harm' (I.3.122). This foresight is amply fulfilled later. Perhaps even more importantly, though, in terms of his character, is the way he resists the temptation to do evil – whereas Macbeth is immediately tempted by the witches' words, Banquo resists them. And it is resistance that is the hallmark of his attitude to the prophecies – they seem to pursue him (since they cannot in his waking thoughts) into his sleep. But there, awoken, he exclaims, 'Merciful powers,/Restrain in me the cursèd thoughts that nature/Gives way to in repose' (II.1.7–9). Calling on heavenly powers to preserve him from evil is quite contrary to Macbeth asking the stars to go out in order to hide his intentions, or Lady Macbeth invoking demons. Banquo is man of integrity – a man who has chosen to do good, and this whatever the cost. As he says to Macbeth, who sounds him out prior to the murder, he will 'keep/My bosom franchised and allegiance clear' (II.1.27-8). There can be no compromise of honour. It is interesting to note, in the context of his rejection of the supernatural revelations, Banquo is a keen lover of nature (I.6.3–9).

If there is a weakness in Banquo's character it might be located in his failure to act. Why does he not reveal what he knows about the prophecies immediately following the murder of Duncan, especially as he states that he stands against 'treasonous malice' (II.3.129)? That he suspects Macbeth is evident when he says – too late to alter Macbeth's coronation – 'Thou playedst most foully for't' (III.1.3). Failure to act on his suspicions costs him his life. And the failure to realise that – as the only other witness to the witches' prophecies – once Macbeth achieves the throne, his life is in danger is, perhaps, an indication that his 'wisdom' has a very definite limit. Like Duncan, Banquo appears too trusting.

MACDUFF

Fittingly, it is Macduff who discovers Duncan's murdered body, and becomes his avenger. He is a man of strong and emotional convictions. From the start he is suspicious of Macbeth – challenging his killing of the guards, and then abstaining from the coronation at Scone. Later he refuses to attend the banquet, and this leads to the murder of his family. Perhaps in this and in his flight to England we see two aspects of his character: we see what Malcolm calls 'this noble passion/Child of integrity' (IV.3.114–15) and alongside this the question of Macduff's judgement. Lady Macduff considers his flight cowardice; Malcolm initially finds it so difficult to accept that he treats Macduff with extreme suspicion. Was it the right thing to do? Perhaps we might argue that for Macduff the affairs of state were more important than family considerations, but this would be to suggest that he was calculating in some sort of political way. It seems

Strong
Suspicious
Brave
Open
Loyal
Forthright

more likely that Macduff is a character who is passionate for justice, and being swept along in the train of events – and his flight to England – simply did not foresee the extent of savagery that Macbeth would exercise on Macduff's family.

However we interpret his flight, one thing is clear – his deep and passionate attachment and love for his family. His reaction to their deaths is one of the most moving scenes in the play. Haunted by their ghosts, he determines to kill Macbeth – and here too we see the compassion of the man who, in the heat of battle, disdains to strike 'wretched kerns' (V.6.27). They are not responsible – Macbeth is. With a sole and bloody purpose, equal to that of Macbeth's, Macduff confronts his enemy and proves his courage and his strength.

MINOR CHARACTERS

Malcolm and
Donalbain

Once they flee after their father's death, we only meet Malcolm again. Their presence together, though, particularly praying as Macbeth is committing the murder, reinforces our sense of brotherly love and of a close knit family unit. Duncan isn't only a good king, but also a good family man. Malcolm emerges as similar to his father, although his harrowing experience escaping from Macbeth's clutches possibly makes him more astute: the testing of Macduff shows a desire to want to penetrate beyond the face to the mind's construction. But he is innocent in the sense of being inexperienced (so youthful) and also in the sense of being free from vice. However, he is dignified, determined, brave, recognises the worth of others, and can take advice. These qualities bode well for his future reign.

Lady Macduff	She appears in only one, yet highly affecting, scene. But we notice her anger, her wit and her courage. Her fate – and her husband not being present to protect her – must appear to her beyond all reason. There is in both the Lady Macduff and Malcolm with Donalbain scenes a sharp contrast when we reflect on Macbeth's 'family' scenes with his wife (and their content), and on the fact that it is the prophesied lack of an heir to the throne that so troubles Macbeth.
Ross	Ross is mostly a messenger, albeit a highly ranked one – he informs Macbeth he is Thane of Cawdor; and he informs Macduff of his wife's murder. But through all these courtesies, one cannot help but feel that Ross believes in self help. He is at the banquet and requests Macbeth's 'royal company' (III.4.44), and although he warns Lady Macduff – 'dearest cuz' (IV.2.14) – he slips himself safely away.
Lennox and Seyward	Lennox is a courtier who suspects Macbeth early on, although he serves him initially. As and when he can, he switches sides to fight against Macbeth. Seyward is a fine soldier, who leads the English army. Shakespeare invests him with a convincing moment of pathos (see Literary Terms) when he learns of the death of his son.
The Old Man and the Porter	The Old Man is a typical Shakespearean creation. He acts as a chorus or commentary on the action: his longevity gives him the right to comment on exactly how unnatural the proceedings have been. The fact that he is old is in itself natural – Macbeth cannot look for 'old age' (V.3.24). The Porter is a marvellous lowlife type of character – drunk, obscene, garrulous. The marvel is in how Shakespeare bends even the Porter's language to serve the themes of the play – whilst simultaneously giving Macbeth an opportunity to wash and change clothing before reappearing on stage.

Y

The Witches   We have already raised the question of whether the
witches are human at all, and if so whether they can be
considered, therefore, to have characters. There can be
no definitive answer. Suffice to say, they embody a
malign and demonic intelligence. This, of necessity, is
fixed and elemental. Their information does tempt
Macbeth – but it must be remembered: they do not
invite him to murder Duncan or even suggest such a
thing. Information is morally neutral until human
beings begin to interpret it. Thus they symbolise (see
Literary Terms) evil, but man is free to resist them.
Macbeth is tragic (see Literary Terms) partly because
he comes to depend upon their information.

LANGUAGE & STYLE

Macbeth is one of Shakespeare's mature tragedies (see
Literary Terms) – it was written at the height of his
powers. It is no surprise, therefore, to discover that the
language of the play is rich and varied. There are three
forms of language to consider: blank verse, prose and
verse couplets (see Literary Terms). Furthermore,
comment needs to be made on imagery and symbolism
(see Literary Terms) in the play.

Blank verse   Blank verse (sometimes called iambic pentameter – see
Literary Terms) is the expressive medium in which
most of the play is written. It can perform any number
of functions: from a bald statement of fact (V.5.16) to
the skilful dialectic (see Literary Terms) between
Malcolm and Macduff (IV.3); from the impassioned
soliloquy (see Literary Terms) and invocation to
demons (I.5) to a weary resignation and despair of life
(V.5). Blank verse is flexible and its rhythms seem to
reflect whatever mood Shakespeare is trying to capture
in the character. One way that Shakespeare achieves his
effects is through his choice of diction (see Literary

Terms). A good example of this would be: 'No, this my hand will rather/The multitudinous seas incarnadine/Making the green one red' (II.2.61–3). Here the polysyllabic, latin-like vocabulary of 'multitudinous' and 'incarnadine' contrasts starkly with the monosyllabic simplicity of 'green one red'. Macbeth's mind wrestles with the enormity of his crime – the inflated diction and its accompanying, sonorous rhythms reflects this enormity; and then switches to a direct and simple fact – for all the enormity of the sea, his bloody hand will turn it red. One listens to the effects; and one studies the choice of words.

Prose

Prose is used in several scenes, most notably in the letter to Lady Macbeth (I.5), the Porter scene (II.3), the murder of Lady Macduff and her son (IV.2) and the sleepwalking of Lady Macbeth (V.1). In each case prose seems entirely appropriate for the task in hand. The letter to Lady Macbeth is concise yet interesting for what it omits to say. The Porter scene leads to the general observation that Shakespeare frequently used prose when dealing with characters of a lower social standing. Blank verse is more 'noble' or elevated and so for nobler characters. Thus, there almost seems a pattern in its use in Macbeth: namely, it does seem to indicate a falling away from nobility or perfection. Lady Macbeth reads the letter and immediately invokes demons and plans murder. Later, she speaks prose when she is mentally disorientated. Lady Macduff begins by speaking in blank verse but as the pressure on her increases prose takes over. She regains the power of blank verse – and so dignity – as she confronts the murderers. As for the Porter, his speech is quite overtly obscene as well as being an ordinary – but drunk – person's commentary on the 'hell' of a place he is in.

Verse couplets

Verse couplets are used in two important ways. The witches use them in their conversation, and this is entirely appropriate as it suggests the world of spells and incantations. Frequently, too, characters conclude a scene with a couplet. This indicates the end of the scene, but also, and often, points to a central idea. For example, the bell, for Duncan, rings heaven or hell (II.1.64). The word 'hell' here – rhyming as it does – has extra resonance and depth.

Words
It is instructive to look at the language Shakespeare uses. Some literal words are constantly repeated to hammer home their importance to the meaning of the play. The repetition creates a dense texture. Words like 'done' (ironically – see Literary Terms – the sense of being undone never far from such doings in the case of Macbeth), 'won', 'lost', 'fair', 'foul'. Other words, sometimes literal, sometimes figurative (see Literary Terms) become, through their associations, part of the rich imagery (see Literary Terms) of the play: blood, dark, light, feasting, clothing and children. Because these words and ideas are constantly being explored and exploited, the net effect is to create a wealth of nuances and meanings, ambiguities and insights.

Symbolism
The symbolism (see Literary Terms) of the play is seamlessly connected with the imagery (see Literary Terms): blood, for example, operates on at least three levels – it is what is literally shed when wars and murders occur; it is also part of the imagery that pervades the play, creating a sense of menace and destruction; and it is a symbol for the evil that is associated with Macbeth. It is important in terms of the symbols to remember the Christian and Biblical context in which the play was written. Even Macbeth acknowledges heaven and hell, and the references to light and dark, nature and the unnatural, often allude to the great Christian symbols – the crucifixion, for example, is not only an event, but a symbolic one, and it has its parallels in *Macbeth*.

PART FOUR

STUDY SKILLS

HOW TO USE QUOTATIONS

One of the secrets of success in writing essays is the way you use quotations. There are five basic principles:

- Put inverted commas at the beginning and end of the quotation
- Write the quotation exactly as it appears in the original
- Do not use a quotation that repeats what you have just written
- Use the quotation so that it fits into your sentence
- Keep the quotation as short as possible

Quotations should be used to develop the line of thought in your essays.

Your comment should not duplicate what is in your quotation. For example:

> **Lady Macbeth tells us that she wants her husband to arrive speedily so that she can pour her spirits in his ear, 'Hie thee hither/That I may pour my spirits in thine ear'.**

Far more effective is to write:

> **Lady Macbeth tells her husband to arrive speedily so that 'I may pour my spirits in thine ear'.**

Always lay out the lines as they appear in the text. For example:

> **Lady Macbeth is immediately ambitious for her husband,**
> **'... and shalt be/What thou art promised'**

or:

> **Lady Macbeth is immediately ambitious for her husband,**
> **'... and shalt be**
> **What thou art promised'**

However, the most sophisticated way of using the writer's words is to embed them into your sentence:

> **The fact that Lady Macbeth may 'read strange matters' in Macbeth's face shows how well she knows his character.**

When you use quotations in this way, you are demonstrating the ability to use text as evidence to support your ideas.

Everyone writes differently. Work through the suggestions given here and adapt the advice to suit your own style and interests. This will improve your essay-writing skills and allow your personal voice to emerge.

The following points indicate in ascending order the skills of essay writing:

- Picking out one or two facts about the story and adding the odd detail
- Writing about the text by retelling the story
- Retelling the story and adding a quotation here and there
- Organising an answer which explains what is happening in the text and giving quotations to support what you write

....

- Writing in such a way as to show that you have thought about the intentions of the writer of the text and that you understand the techniques used
- Writing at some length, giving your viewpoint on the text and commenting by picking out details to support your views
- Looking at the text as a work of art, demonstrating clear critical judgement and explaining to the reader of your essay how the enjoyment of the text is assisted by literary devices, linguistic effects and psychological insights; showing how the text relates to the time when it was written

The dotted line above represents the division between lower and higher level grades. Higher-level performance begins when you start to consider your response as a reader of the text. The highest level is reached when you offer an enthusiastic personal response and show how this piece of literature is a product of its time.

Coursework essay

Set aside an hour or so at the start of your work to plan what you have to do.

- List all the points you feel are needed to cover the task. Collect page references of information and quotations that will support what you have to say. A helpful tool is the highlighter pen: this saves painstaking copying and enables you to target precisely what you want to use.
- Focus on what you consider to be the main points of the essay. Try to sum up your argument in a single sentence, which could be the closing sentence of your essay. Depending on the essay title, it could be a statement about a character: Macbeth, despite the evil he commits, is nevertheless a courageous soldier; an opinion about setting: Macbeth's decision to leave the security of his castle because the wood has moved is a fatal irony; or a judgement on a theme: I think that the main theme of *Macbeth* is ambition because it is this vice, more than any other, that leads Macbeth to violate his own conscience and so set in motion the whole deadly series of events.
- Make a short essay plan. Use the first paragraph to introduce the argument you wish to make. In the following paragraphs develop this argument with details, examples and other possible points of view. Sum up your argument in the last paragraph. Check you have answered the question.
- Write the essay, remembering all the time the central point you are making.
- On completion, go back over what you have written to eliminate careless errors and improve expression. Read it aloud to yourself, or, if you are feeling more confident, to a relative or friend.

If you can, try to type your essay using a word processor. This will allow you to correct and improve your writing without spoiling its appearance.

Examination essay

The essay written in an examination often carries more marks than the coursework essay even though it is written under considerable time pressure.

In the revision period build up notes on various aspects of the text you are using. Fortunately, in acquiring this set of York Notes on *Macbeth*, you have made a prudent beginning! York Notes are set out to give you vital information and help you to construct your personal overview of the text.

Make notes with appropriate quotations about the key issues of the set text. Go into the examination knowing your text and having a clear set of opinions about it.

In most English Literature examinations you can take in copies of your set books. This in an enormous advantage although it may lull you into a false sense of security. Beware! There is simply not enough time in an examination to read the book from scratch.

In the examination

- Read the question paper carefully and remind yourself what you have to do.
- Look at the questions on your set texts to select the one that most interests you and mentally work out the points you wish to stress.
- Remind yourself of the time available and how you are going to use it.
- Briefly map out a short plan in note form that will keep your writing on track and illustrate the key argument you want to make.
- Then set about writing it.
- When you have finished, check through to eliminate errors.

To summarise, these are keys to success

- **Know the text**
- **Have a clear understanding of and opinions on the storyline, characters, setting, themes and writer's concerns**
- **Select the right material**
- **Plan and write a clear response, continually bearing the question in mind**

A typical essay question on *Macbeth* is followed by a sample essay plan in note form. This does not present the only answer to the question, merely one answer. Do not be afraid to include your own ideas and leave out some of the ones in this sample! Remember that quotations are essential to prove and illustrate the points you make.

Macbeth – tyrant or tragic hero? Discuss.

The Plan

It is vital in undertaking a question that one breaks it down into smaller units, and then tackles each unit systematically. Discussion of the above question suggests at least four areas that must be covered:

1 what distinctions can be made between a tyrant and a tragic hero?
2 evidence to support *both* positions
3 clear indications as to which points are the most significant
4 reasons for your final opinion

Let us look at these four points in turn.

Part 1

In looking at distinctions between a tyrant and a tragic hero we need to define what *each* is. For example:

Tyrant	Tragic Hero
all-powerful, totalitarian	courageous
ruthless	weak, having a weakness
cruel and arbitrary	driven by other forces
capricious	beyond his control
unsympathetic	sympathetic
lacking imagination	imaginative but trapped

Part 2

We now need to link *words* and *actions* to these distinctions. For example:

'all-powerful and totalitarian':

Words: he says, 'I could with bare-faced power sweep him from my sight' (III.1.117), although he decides to have Banquo murdered instead.

Actions: the destruction of Macduff's family (IV.2).

Similarly, we can take 'courageous' in order to establish a more favourable response to Macbeth's character. It is not necessary to alternate the points, as the list does. One can choose to discuss the words and actions relevant to tyrant in a block, and then do the same for tragic hero. The important thing is to be comfortable with the way one has decided to present the evidence.

Part 3   It is important to indicate the relative worth of the various points one is making. Courage, for example, is a very important point: when we initially meet Macbeth he is defined by his courage, and when we last see him it is his courage which is at stake; it is also the issue of his manhood – his courage – on which Lady Macbeth tempts and persuades him. Therefore any assessment of Macbeth must address this issue.

Part 4   The final point is linked to part 3. Tyrant or tragic hero partly depends on the relative weighting of the evidence. It may be that he is both. Be sure, however, to balance your evidence.

Conclusion   The key aspect of reaching a conclusion is to accept the evidence which seems to contradict your conclusion, but then to show why it is not so valid. A good example of this might be if one concluded that Macbeth were more tyrant than tragic hero. The courage he shows in facing Macduff in the final scene does, however, suggest a hero. Therefore, to counter this one might present alternative explanations: true, he faces Macduff but not because he is courageous – but because, perhaps, he was more frightened of public abuse, or perhaps he faced him not out of courage but out of that same dogged devotion to prophecy that he had previously shown – he had to die then because the witches had said so. These explanations may or may not be strained, but the general principle is clear:

- look at all the evidence
- weigh it up
- decide which pieces of it are the most compelling and why the counter evidence is less so

When that is done, the conclusion is likely to be convincing.

FURTHER QUESTIONS

Make a plan as shown above and attempt these questions.

1 Choose a scene from *Macbeth* which you think is a turning point. Write about this scene bringing out its importance in the play as a whole.
2 Write about a major theme of the play *Macbeth*.
3 Write about the impact the character of Lady Macbeth has on the reader/audience.
4 Write about Shakespeare's use of imagery in *Macbeth* with particular reference to two or three major images.

PART FIVE

CULTURAL CONNECTIONS

BROADER PERSPECTIVES

Macbeth is one of Shakespeare's most popular plays and has had a tremendous cultural influence. It drives home its points relentlessly; and its combination of character, action and the supernatural mean it is enduringly fascinating. As a result *Macbeth* has appeared in many different media.

Music

Probably the most famous musical adaptation of *Macbeth* is Verdi's opera *Macbeth* (1847). Richard Strauss also wrote a symphonic poem called *Macbeth* (1890).

Film

There have been at least seventeen film versions of *Macbeth*. Akira Kurosawa's adaptation, *Throne of Blood* (1957) is considered the best and Ken Hughe's *Joe Macbeth* (1956) is a fascinating gangster version. Nearer home, two versions that are extremely good are the Trevor Nunn TV version (1976) and the Roman Polanski film (1971).

Novels

The topicality of *Macbeth*'s central theme – ambition – means that it relects effortlessly on much history, contemporay or otherwise. For example, in George Orwell's *Animal farm* (Longman, 1991 – first published 1945), The ruthless ambition of Napoleon parallels that of Macbeth. Susan Hill's *I'm the King of the Castle* (Longman, 1981 – first published 1970) shows the jealousies in the relationship between two boys.

Poetry

Recent poets you may want to study include W.B. Yeats and Dylan Thomas. For example, 'The Second Coming' by W.B. Yeats (*Selected Poetry*, Macmillan, 1971) creates a terrifying sense of evil and menace. Dylan Thomas wrote 'The Force That Through the Green Fuse Dries the Flower' (*Collected Poems* 1934–52, Dent, 1974) evokes an elemental world in which the power of life is also its destroyer.

Y

blank verse unrhymed iambic pentameter a line of five iambs

couplet a pair of rhymed lines of any metre – so Verse Couplet

dialectic logical disputation; investigation of truth by discussion

diction the choice of words in a work of fiction; the kind of vocabulary used

doggerel bad verse – ill-constructed, rough, clumsy versification

dramatic irony when the development of the plot allows the audience to possess more information about what is happening than some of the characters themselves have

epithet adjective or adjectival phrase which defines a special quality or attribute

figurative any form of expression which deviates from the plainest expression of meaning

iambic consisting of the iamb – which is the commonest metrical foot in English verse. It has two syllables, consisting of one weak stress followed by a strong stress, ti-tum

imagery its narrowest meaning is a word-picture. More commonly, imagery refers to figurative language in which words that refer to objects and qualities appeal to the senses and the feelings. Often imagery is expressed through metaphor

irony saying one thing when another is meant

metaphor a comparison in which one thing is said (or implied) to be another

metonymy the substitution of the name of a thing by the name of an attribute of it e.g. the Crown for the monarchy

motif some aspect of literature (a type of character, theme or image) which recurs frequently

naturalism a particular branch of realism – it concentrates on presenting life without a spiritual dimension

pathos moments in a work of art which evoke strong feelings of pity and sorrow

pentameter in versification a line of five feet – often iambic

personifications a metaphor in which things or ideas are treated as if they were human beings, with human attributes and feelings

prose any language that is not made patterned by the regularity of metre

pun a play on words in which two different meanings – often contrasting – are drawn from the same word

soliloquy a dramatic convention allowing a character to speak directly to the audience, as if thinking aloud their thoughts and feelings

sonnet a lyric poem of fixed form, usually fourteen lines with an intricate rhyme pattern

symbol something which represents something else e.g. a rose standing for beauty

synecdoche a figure of speech in which a part is used to describe the whole of something e.g. 'all hands on deck' where hands clearly refers to sailors

tragedy basically, tragedy traces the career and downfall of an individual and shows in this downfall both the capacities and limitations of human life

TEST ANSWERS

TEST YOURSELF (Act I)

A···
1 The witches *(Scene 1)*
2 Duncan *(Scene 2)*
3 Macbeth *(Scene 3)*
4 Malcolm *(Scene 4)*
5 Lady Macbeth *(Scene 5)*
6 Banquo *(Scene 6)*
7 Macbeth *(Scene 7)*
8 Macdonwald *(Scene 2)*
9 Macbeth *(Scene 2)*
10 Macbeth *(Scene 4)*
11 Lady Macbeth *(Scene 6)*

TEST YOURSELF (Act II)

A···
1 Banquo *(Scene 1)*
2 Macbeth *(Scene 1)*
3 Lady Macbeth *(Scene 2)*
4 A voice Macbeth says he hears *(Scene 2)*
5 Lady Macbeth *(Scene 2)*
6 Macduff *(Scene 3)*
7 Macbeth *(Scene 3)*
8 Duncan *(Scene 2)*
9 Malcolm and Donalbain *(Scene 2)*
10 The grooms/guards of Duncan *(Scene 2)*
11 Lady Macbeth *(Scene 3)*
12 Donalbain *(Scene 3)*
13 Macbeth *(Scene 4)*

TEST YOURSELF (Act III)

A···
1 Banquo *(Scene 1)*
2 Macbeth *(Scene 1)*
3 First Murderer *(Scene 1)*
4 Macbeth *(Scene 2)*
5 Lady Macbeth *(Scene 2)*
6 Ross *(Scene 4)*
7 Macbeth *(Scene 4)*
8 Hecate *(Scene 5)*
9 Lennox *(Scene 6)*

10 Malcolm and Donalbain *(Scene 7)*
11 Banquo *(Scene 7)*
12 The murderers *(Scene 2)*
13 Macbeth *(Scene 2)*
14 Macduff *(Scene 4)*
15 Macbeth *(Scene 6)*

TEST YOURSELF (Act IV)

A···
1 First Witch *(Scene 1)*
2 Macbeth *(Scene 2)*
3 Lady Macduff *(Scene 2)*
4 Macduff *(Scene 3)*
5 Malcolm *(Scene 3)*
6 Macduff *(Scene 3)*
7 Malcolm *(Scene 3)*
8 The witches *(Scene 1)*
9 Macduff *(Scene 2)*
10 Macduff *(Scene 3)*
11 Macduff *(Scene 3)*
12 Edward, King of England *(Scene 3)*

TEST YOURSELF (Act V)

A···
1 Lady Macbeth *(Scene 1)*
2 Doctor *(Scene 1)*
3 Angus *(Scene 2)*
4 Macbeth *(Scene 3)*
5 Malcolm *(Scene 4)*
6 Macbeth *(Scene 5)*
7 Macduff *(Scene 6)*
8 Seyward *(Scene 6)*
9 Malcolm *(Scene 6)*
10 Lady Macbeth *(Scene 1)*
11 Macbeth *(Scene 2)*
12 Macbeth *(Scene 6)*
13 Young Seyward *(Scene 6)*

GCSE and equivalent levels (£3.50 each)

Harold Brighouse
Hobson's Choice

Charles Dickens
Great Expectations

Charles Dickens
Hard Times

George Eliot
Silas Marner

William Golding
Lord of the Flies

Thomas Hardy
The Mayor of Casterbridge

Susan Hill
I'm the King of the Castle

Barry Hines
A Kestrel for a Knave

Harper Lee
To Kill a Mockingbird

Arthur Miller
A View from the Bridge

Arthur Miller
The Crucible

George Orwell
Animal Farm

J.B. Priestley
An Inspector Calls

J.D. Salinger
The Catcher in the Rye

William Shakespeare
Macbeth

William Shakespeare
The Merchant of Venice

William Shakespeare
Romeo and Juliet

William Shakespeare
Twelfth Night

George Bernard Shaw
Pygmalion

John Steinbeck
Of Mice and Men

Mildred D. Taylor
Roll of Thunder, Hear My Cry

James Watson
Talking in Whispers

A Choice of Poets

Nineteenth Century Short Stories

Poetry of the First World War

FORTHCOMING TITLES IN THE SERIES

Advanced level (£3.99 each)

Margaret Atwood
The Handmaid's Tale

Jane Austen
Emma

Jane Austen
Pride and Prejudice

William Blake
Poems/Songs of Innocence and Songs of Experience

Emily Brontë
Wuthering Heights

Geoffrey Chaucer
Wife of Bath's Prologue and Tale

Joseph Conrad
Heart of Darkness

Charles Dickens
Great Expectations

F. Scott Fitzgerald
The Great Gatsby

Thomas Hardy
Tess of the D'Urbervilles

Seamus Heaney
Selected Poems

James Joyce
Dubliners

William Shakespeare
Antony and Cleopatra

William Shakespeare
Hamlet

William Shakespeare
King Lear

William Shakespeare
Macbeth

William Shakespeare
Othello

Mary Shelley
Frankenstein

Alice Walker
The Color Purple

John Webster
The Duchess of Malfi

York Notes – the Ultimate Literature Guides

York Notes are recognised as the best literature study guides.
If you have enjoyed using this book and have found it useful, you
can now order others directly from us – simply follow the ordering
instructions below.

HOW TO ORDER

Decide which title(s) you require and then order in one of the following
ways:

Booksellers
All titles available from good bookstores.

By post
List the title(s) you require in the space provided overleaf,
select your method of payment, complete your name and
address details and return your completed order form and
payment to:

Addison Wesley Longman Ltd
PO BOX 88
Harlow
Essex CM19 5SR

By phone
Call our Customer Information Centre on 01279 623923 to
place your order, quoting mail number: HEYN1.

By fax
Complete the order form overleaf, ensuring you fill in your
name and address details and method of payment, and fax it
to us on 01279 414130.

By e-mail
E-mail your order to us on awlhe.orders@awl.co.uk listing
title(s) and quantity required and providing full name and
address details as requested overleaf. Please
quote mail number: HEYN1. Please do not
send credit card details by e-mail.

York Notes Order Form

Titles required:

Quantity	Title/ISBN	Price

Sub total _____

Please add £2.50 postage & packing _____

(*P & P is free for orders over £50*) _____

Total _____

Mail no: HEYN1

Your Name _____

Your Address _____

Postcode _____   Telephone _____

Method of payment

☐ I enclose a cheque or a P/O for £_____ made payable to Addison Wesley Longman Ltd

☐ Please charge my Visa/Access/AMEX/Diners Club card
Number _____   Expiry Date _____
Signature _____   Date _____

(please ensure that the address given above is the same as for your credit card)

Prices and other details are correct at time of going to press but may change without notice. All orders are subject to status.

☐ *Please tick this box if you would like a complete listing of Longman Study Guides (suitable for GCSE and A-level students)*

York Press

Longman

Addison Wesley Longman